W9-AZY-285

Master Reading is designed to help children improve reading skills while expanding their reading vocabulary. In addition to introducing new sight words and providing practice in fundamental skills such as classifying and sequencing, these activities offer children practice in understanding what they read through practical reading exercises.

Table of Contents

Glossary

Analogy. A way of comparing things to show how they relate. For example: nose is to smell as tongue is to taste.

Classifying. Putting similar things into categories.

Context. A way to figure out the meaning of a new word by relating it to the other words in the sentence.

Fact. Information that can be proved. Example: Hawaii is a state.

Homographs. Words that have the same spelling but different meaning and pronunciations.

Idioms. A phrase that says one thing but actually means something quite different. Example: Now that's <u>a horse of a different color</u>!

Inference. Using logic to figure out what is unspoken but evident.

Main Idea. Finding the most important points.

Opinion. Information that tells what someone thinks. It cannot be proved. Example: Hawaii is the prettiest state.

Prefix. A syllable at the beginning of a word that changes its meaning.

Scan. Looking for certain words in a reading selection to locate facts or answer questions.

Sequencing. Putting things in logical order.

Similes. Comparing two things that have something in common but are really very different. The words **like** and **as** are used in similes. Example: The baby was <u>as happy as a lark.</u>

Skim. Reading quickly to get a general idea of what a reading selection is about.

Suffix. A syllable at the end of a word that changes its meaning.

Syllable. Word divisions. Each syllable has one vowel sound.

Syllabication. Dividing words into parts, each with a vowel sound.

Name: _____

Adding Suffixes

The suffixes **-ant** and **-ent** mean a person or thing that does something. Example, one who occupies a place is the occup**ant**.

Directions: Combine each root word and suffix to make a new word. (When a word ends in silent **e**, keep the **e** before adding a suffix beginning with a consonant. Drop the **e** before adding a suffix beginning with a vowel.)

Example: announce + ment = announcement; announce + ing + announcing.) The first one is done for you.

ROOT WORD	SUFFIX	NEW WORD
observe	-ant	observant
contest	-ant	_____
please	-ant	_____
preside	-ent	_____
differ	-ent	_____

Directions: Using the meanings in the parentheses, complete each sentence with one of the words you just formed. One is done for you.

1. To be a good scientist you must be very _observant_, (pay careful attention)

2. Her perfume had a strong but very _____ smell. (pleasing)

3. Because the bridge was out, we had to find a _____ route home. (not the same)

4. The game show _____ jumped up and down when she won the grand prize. (person who competes in a contest)

5. Next week we will elect a new student council _____. (highest officer)

Name: _____

Make New Words

The suffix **-al** means of, like, or suitable for; **-ative** means having the nature of or relating to; **-ive** means have or tend to be.

Directions: Combine each root word and suffix to form a new word. Remember that the spelling of the root word sometimes changes when a suffix is added. The first one is done for you.

ROOT WORD	SUFFIX	NEW WORD
logic	-al	logical
imagine	-ative	_____
talk	-ative	_____
impress	-ive	_____
attract	-ive	_____

Directions: Using the meanings in the parentheses, complete each sentence with one of the words you just formed.

1. Because of his acting ability, Michael was the _____ choice to have the lead part in the school play. (decided with reasoning)

2. Our history teacher is a rather _____ man, who likes to tell jokes and stories. (fond of talking)

3. That book has such an _____ plot! (showing imagination)

4. Monica thought the dress in the store window was very

   _____. (pleasing, something that attracts)

5. The high school basketball team was _____ in its Friday night game, beating their rivals by thirty points. (making an impression on the mind or emotions)

Name: _____

Changing The Meanings Of Words

The prefixes **il-**, **im-**, **in-**, and **ir-** all mean not.

Directions: Divide each word into its prefix and root word. The first one is done for you.

	PREFIX	ROOT WORD
illogical	il	logic
impatient	_____	_____
immature	_____	_____
incomplete	_____	_____
insincere	_____	_____
irresponsible	_____	_____
irregular	_____	_____

Directions: Using the meanings in the parentheses, complete each sentence with one of the words you just formed.

1. I had to turn in my assignment _____ because I was sick last night. (not finished)

2. It was _____ for Jimmy to give me his keys because he can't get into his house without them. (not reasonable)

3. Sue and Joel were _____ to have a party while there parents were out of town. (lacking a sense of responsiblity)

4. I sometimes get _____ waiting for my ride to school. (a lack of patience)

5. The boys sounded _____ when they said they were sorry. (not honest)

6. These pants didn't cost much because they are _____ . (not straight or even)

Name: _____

Homographs

Directions: Write the definition from the box for the bold word in each sentence.

pres ent	*n.*	a gift
pre sent	*v.*	to introduce or offer to view
rec ord	*n.*	written or official evidence
re cord	*v.*	to keep an account of
wind	*n.*	air in motion
wind	*v.*	to tighten the spring by turning a knob, as with a watch
wound (woond)	*n.*	an injury in which the skin is broken
wound	*v.*	past tense of wind

1. I would like to **present** our new student council president, Mindy Hall.

_____

2. The store made a **record** of all my payments.

_____

3. Don't forget to **wind** your alarm clock before you go to sleep.

_____

4. He received a serious **wound** on his hand by playing with a knife.

_____

5. The **wind** knocked over my bicycle.

_____

6. I bought her a birthday **present** with my allowance.

_____

Name: _____

What Is The Correct Meaning?

Directions: Circle the correct definition of the bold word in each sentence. One is done for you.

1. Try to **flag** down a car to get us some help!

   to signal to stop
   cloth used as symbol

2. We listened to the **band** play the National Anthem.

   group of musicians
   a binding or tie

3. He was the **sole** survivor of the plane crash.

   bottom of the foot
   one and only

4. I am going to **pound** the nail with this hammer.

   to hit hard
   a unit of weight

5. He lived on what little **game** he could find in the woods.

   animals for hunting
   form of entertainment

6. We are going to **book** the midnight flight from Miami.

   to reserve in advance
   a literary work

7. The **pitcher** looked toward first base before throwing the ball.

   baseball team member
   container for pouring

8. My grandfather and I played a **game** of checkers last night.

   animals for hunting
   form of entertainment

9. They raise the **flag** over City Hall every morning.

   to signal to stop
   cloth used as symbol

Name: _____

Similes

Directions: Choose a word from the word box to complete each comparison. One is done for you.

tack	grass	fish	mule	ox	rail	hornet	monkey

1. as stubborn as a _____mule_____

2. as strong as an _____

3. swims like a _____

4. as sharp as a _____

5. as thin as a _____

6. as mad as a _____

7. climbs like a _____

8. as green as _____

Directions: Use words of your own to complete the following similes.

1. as _____ as a tack

2. as light as a _____

3. _____ like a bird

4. as _____ as honey

5. as hungry as a _____

6. _____ like a snake

7. as white as _____

8. as cold as _____

Directions: Make up similes to finish the following sentences.

1. Our new puppy sounded _____.

2. The clouds were _____.

3. Our new car is _____.

4. The watermelon tasted _____.

Name: _____

Figurative Language

Directions: Write the letter of the correct meaning for the bold words in each sentence. One is done for you.

a. refusal to see or listen	**f**. pay for
b. misbehaving, acting in a wild way	**g**. unknowing
c. made a thoughtless remark	**h**. feeling very sad
d. lost an opportunity	**i**. get married
e. got angry	**j**. excited and happy

___f___ 1. My parents will **foot the bill** for my birthday party.

_____ 2. Tony and Lisa will finally **tie the knot** in June.

_____ 3. Sam was **down in the dumps** after he wrecked his bicycle.

_____ 4. Sarah **put her foot in her mouth** when she was talking to our teacher.

_____ 5. I really **missed the boat** when I turned down the chance to work after school.

_____ 6. I got the **brush off** from Susan when I tried to ask her where she was last night.

_____ 7. Mickey is **in the dark** about our plans to throw a surprise birthday party for him.

_____ 8. The children were **bouncing off the walls** when the babysitter was trying to put them to bed.

_____ 9. The students were **flying high** on the last day of school.

_____ 10. My sister **lost her cool** when she found out that I spilled chocolate milk on her new sweater.

Name: _____

Review

Directions: Circle the word or phrase that best defines the bold words in each sentence.

1. The woman had a very **pleasant** voice.
   loud
   one that pleases
   strange

2. The **central** regions of the country suffer most from the drought.
   hottest
   southern
   of or near the center

3. He had a very **imaginative** excuse for not turning in his homework.
   relating to the imagination
   difficult to believe
   acceptable

4. I didn't get credit for my answer on the test because it was **incomplete**.
   not correct
   too short
   not finished

5. Will you **wind** the music box for the baby?
   air in motion
   an injury in which the skin is broken
   to tighten the spring by turning a knob

6. To enroll in the school, you must bring your birth certificate or some other legal **record** for identification.
   to keep an account
   a flat disk that plays music
   written or official evidence

7. We use the crystal **pitcher** when we have company.
   a printed likeness of a person or object
   a baseball team member
   a container for pouring

8. This block is **as light as a feather!**
   very heavy
   not heavy at all
   can be put in a cage

9. The whole family was there when Bill and Lynn **tied the knot** last weekend.
   were caught in a trap
   bought a house
   got married

10. I will have to **foot the bill** for the damage you caused.
    kick
    pay for
    seek payment

11. Carol **lost her cool** when the party was called off.
    got angry
    had a fever
    went home

12. The kite **soared like an eagle**.
    flapped and fluttered
    glided along high in the air
    crashed to the ground

Name: _____

Find The Words

Directions: Find each of the words from the word box in the puzzle. Some words go across, some go up and down, one is on the diagonal, and two are backwards. One is done for you.

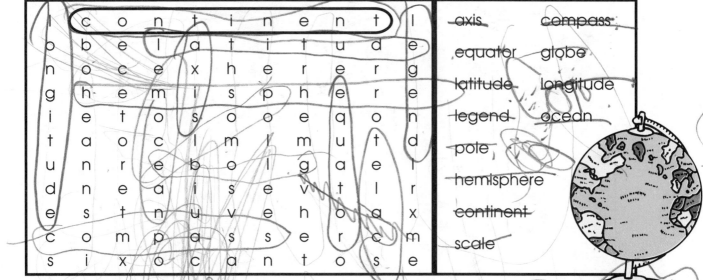

l	c	o	n	t	i	n	e	n	t	l
o	b	e	l	a	t	i	t	u	d	e
n	o	c	e	x	h	e	r	e	r	g
g	h	e	m	i	s	p	h	e	r	e
i	e	t	o	s	o	o	e	q	o	n
t	a	o	c	l	m	l	m	u	t	d
u	n	r	e	b	o	l	g	a	t	e
d	n	e	a	i	s	e	v	h	o	l
e	s	t	n	u	v	e	h	o	a	x
c	o	m	p	a	s	s	e	t	r	m
s	i	x	o	c	a	n	t	o	s	e

axis   compass

equator   globe

latitude   longitude

legend   ocean

pole

hemisphere

continent

scale

Directions: Each sentence tells something about maps but the bold words are jumbled up. Rearrange the letters to spell words from the word box.

1. East and west distances are measured in **gudelnoti**.

2. Half of the earth is called a **premsheehi**.

3. The **quotare** is an imaginary line that divides the earth's surface into the Northern and Southern Hemispheres.

4. Distances north and south of the equator are measured in **iduttale**.

5. The **blego** is the most complete and accurate map of the earth.

6. The **sixa** is an imaginary line on which the earth turns.

7. The seven largest land forms, including Africa, Australia, and North America, are called **cennitonts**.

8. The four largest bodies of water, including the Pacific and the Atlantic, are the **canoes**.

Name: _____

The Continents

Directions: Read the facts about the seven continents and follow the directions.

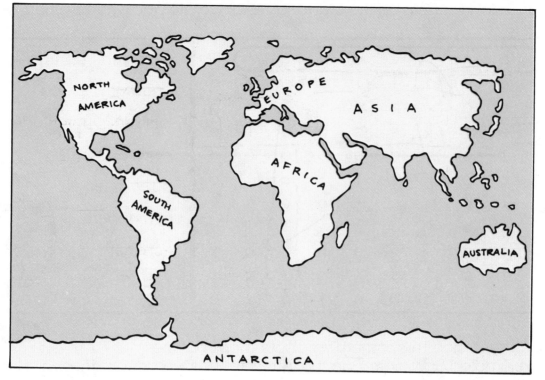

1. **Asia** is the biggest continent. It has the largest land mass and the largest population. Draw a star on Asia.

2. **Africa** is the second largest continent. Put a 2 on Africa.

3. **Australia** is the smallest continent in area: 3 million square miles compared to 17 million square miles for Asia. Write 3,000,000 on Australia.

4. **Australia** is not a very crowded continent. But it does not rank lowest in population. That honor goes to **Antarctica**, which has no permanent population at all! This ice-covered continent is too cold for life. Write ZERO on Antarctica.

5. **Australia** and **Antarctica** are the only continents entirely separated by water. Draw circles around Australia and Antarctica.

6. **North America** and **South America** are joined together by a narrow strip of land. It is called **Central America**. Write an **N** on North America, an **S** on South America, and a **C** on Central America.

7. **Asia** and **Europe** are joined together over such a great distance that they are sometimes called just one continent. The name given it is Eurasia. Draw lines under the names of the two continents in "Eurasia."

Find The State Names

Directions: The name of a state from the word box is hidden in each of the sentences below. Circle it, then draw an X on the state in the map. One is done for you.

Mississippi	Connecticut
Delaware	Maryland
Kentucky	Washington
Ohio	Vermont
Missouri	Illinois
Maine	Alaska

1. I'll be at the airport when Rose (mary land)s the plane for the first time.

2. While her boss is talking, the shy miss is sipping her coffee and listening politely.

3. If the cream is sour, I can't serve it to our guests.

4. They asked me to be quiet, but still I noisily slammed the door.

5. After you fold it, take the washing to Nancy's house.

6. Because I wanted the phone line to disconnect, I cut the wire under the porch.

7. It is sometimes said that when you capture a fortress or citadel, a war ends.

8. When eating chicken, tuck your napkin into your shirt.

9. Meet me after the game at the main entrance to the school.

10. Whenever Monte comes to visit, we have spaghetti for dinner.

11. "Oh, I opened the wrong door!" she said shyly.

12. If you want to know how to care for an animal, ask a librarian to help you find a book on the subject.

Name: _____

Planning A Map

Maps have certain features that help you to read them. For example, a compass points out directions. Color is often used so you can easily see where an area, such as a county, state, or country, stops and the next starts.

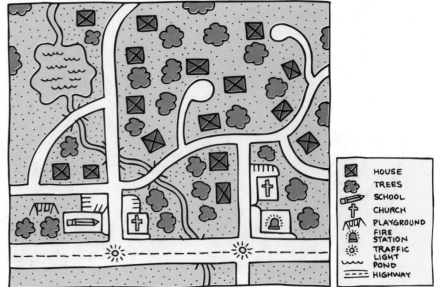

Also, to be accurate, a map must be drawn to scale. The scale of a map shows how much area is represented by a given measurement. It can be small, such as one inch equals one mile, or large, such as one inch equals 1000 miles.

Symbols are another part of the map's language. An airplane may represent an airport. Sometimes a symbol does not look like what it represents. For example, cities are often represented by dots. A legend tells what each symbol means.

One of the best ways to learn about the uses of maps is to make one of your own. You may be surprised at how much you can learn about your neighborhood, too. The only tools you will need are a large piece of paper, a ruler, a pencil, and some colored pencils.

First, choose the area you want to map out. You will then need to decide on the scale for your map. It could be small, such as one inch equals three feet, if you are mapping out your own backyard. For your whole neighborhood, you might have one inch equal to a city block.

You will want to include symbols, such as a picnic table to represent a park or a cross to represent a church. Be sure to include the symbols and other important information in your legend.

Directions: Number in order the steps to making your own map.

____ Figure out the scale that will work best for your map.

____ Gather together a large piece of paper, a ruler, a pencil, and colored pencils.

____ Make a legend explaining the symbols you are using.

____ Draw your map!

____ Draw symbols to represent features of the area you are mapping.

____ Decide on the area you want to map out.

Name: _____

Winter Sleep

In many areas of the world winter weather is very harsh on living things. Plants and animals must find ways to survive the cold temperatures and lack of food and water. Plants and trees drop their leaves and rest. Many birds, some insects, and a few other animals migrate during the winter. Some animals hibernate. Hibernation is sometimes known as "winter sleep."

Mammals that hibernate include woodchucks (which are also called groundhogs), skunks, and some kinds of squirrels, bats, and, of course, bears. To prepare for the winter months, these animals store up fat on their bodies during the summer and fall. They may hide food or take it into their dens or burrows. Some animals line their winter "homes" with grass or hay.

When the temperatures drop, they crawl into their dens. The close space helps to hold in the heat of their bodies. They fall into a deep sleep in which their bodies become almost lifeless. A hibernating bear may rouse itself occasionally and even wander about looking for a new resting place before settling into another deep sleep. The animals use up the stored fat little by little. When they awaken in the spring with the warmer weather, they are thin — and ready for a big meal.

Directions: Number in order the steps a hibernating animal goes through to escape the cold winter weather.

_____ They fall into a deep sleep in which their bodies become almost lifeless.

_____ These animals store up fat on their bodies during the summer and fall.

_____ When the temperatures drop, they crawl into their dens. The close space helps to hold in the heat of their bodies.

_____ When they awaken in the spring with the warmer weather, they are thin — and ready for a big meal.

_____ The animals use up the stored fat little by little.

_____ Some animals hide food or take it into their dens or burrows. They may line their winter "homes" with grass or hay.

Name: _____

Make A Bird Feeder

Bird watching can be fun and educational. By providing for their basic needs — food, water, shelter, and a place to nest — you can attract birds to your own yard, no matter where you live. The easiest way to attract birds is to build a feeder and stock it with food. Here are step-by-step instructions for making a simple one.

The materials you will need are a large tin can (a two-pound coffee can is a good size), a wire coat hanger, a cork, one six-inch aluminum-foil pie pan, and a nine-inch foil pan.

First, using the kind of can opener that cuts small triangles, make five holes in the side of the can right above the bottom rim. Next, straighten the coat hanger and bend one end into a loop. Poke holes the size of the wire in the middle of the two foil pans. Cut another hole in the center of the bottom of the can. Try to make all of the holes in the exact center so they will line up.

With the smaller pan right side up, push the straight end of the wire through its hole and then through the hole in the can. Turn the larger pan upside down and put the wire through its hole. Fill the can with mixed birdseed, making sure that the seed falls through the holes onto the bottom pan. Then force the cork down the wire until it rests tightly against the top pan. Finally, make a hook in the top of the wire to use as a hanger. Hang your feeder where you can easily see it. Sit back and watch for the birds to come!

Directions: Number in order the steps to building the bird feeder.

_____ Cuts holes the size of the wire in the middle of the foil pans and the can.

_____ Fill the can with birdseed and make sure it falls through the holes in the sides of the can onto the bottom pan.

_____ With a can opener, make five openings in the side of the can near the bottom rim.

_____ Form a hook in the end of the wire to use as a hanger.

_____ Gather together a large tin can, two foil pans, a wire coat hanger, and a cork.

_____ Straighten the coat hanger and make a loop in one end.

_____ With the smaller pan turned right side up, push the wire through the holes in the pan and the tin can.

_____ Hang up your bird feeder and watch for the birds to come!

_____ Turn the larger pan upside down and push the wire through the hole.

_____ Force the cork down the wire until it fits tightly against the top plate.

Name: _____

Feed The Birds

Can you imagine feeding birds right from your hand? Here is how you can do just that!

Begin by attracting birds to your windowsill with a bird feeder (such as the one described on page 16). Once they are used to feeding there, you are ready to move to the next part of the plan.

Get a piece of wood that is about two or three feet long and a couple inches wide. Put this "arm" in the sleeve of an old coat or shirt and attach an old glove to the bottom with a thumbtack. Now put the "arm" out of the window over the bird feeder, and close the window to hold it in place. Put some birdseed on the glove every day for a week or so until the birds get used to eating from it.

Next put your own arm and hand inside the sleeve and glove. Rest your arm on the windowsill so it won't get tired and hold some birdseed in your hand. Be very still! After a few days, the birds will get used to eating from your gloved hand. The next step is to take off the glove and put the seed in your bare hand. You will have birds feeding out of your hand in no time!

Directions: Number in order the steps for getting birds to eat from your hand.

_____ Rest your arm on the windowsill and put birdseed in your gloved hand. Hold very still!

_____ Make an "arm" from a piece of wood. Put it inside the sleeve of a coat or shirt and attach an old glove to the bottom.

_____ When the birds become used to eating from your gloved hand, take off the glove.

_____ Stick the "arm" out of the window over the bird feeder and put birdseed in the glove.

_____ Put birdseed in your bare hand and wait for the birds to begin eating right from your hand!

_____ Start attracting birds to your windowsill with a bird feeder. Let them get used to feeding there.

_____ Once the birds are used to feeding from the "arm" you made, put your own hand and arm into the sleeve and glove.

Name: _____

Review

For a long time, people believed that the caterpillar and the butterfly were two unrelated insects. Today, however, we know that they are the same creature at different stages of its development.

This remarkable life cycle begins when the female butterfly lays her eggs — which can number in the hundreds — on a plant that will provide just the right food for the caterpillars that will hatch. The caterpillar begins eating right away and continues to eat constantly. Soon it is too big for its skin. The skin splits to allow the caterpillar to crawl out. This is called molting. The caterpillar may molt as many as ten times before beginning the next stage of development.

During the next stage, called the pupa, there seems to be little activity. In fact, many changes are taking place inside the caterpillar. The caterpillar finds a place, usually on a twig, and deposits a sticky liquid to form a pad. The caterpillar then hangs upside down. The skin molts one final time, leaving the pupa. Immediately, a hard shell called a chrysalis or cocoon is formed.

After 10 to 14 days, the cocoon suddenly bursts open. A few seconds later, the butterfly has come out. At first its wings are pressed together. Fluid is pumped through hollow veins until the wings are fully expanded. The butterfly spreads its wings to dry and harden. Then the fluid is withdrawn from the wing veins. The butterfly is now ready to fly.

Directions: Number in order the stages of a butterfly's life cycle.

_____ A few seconds later, the butterfly has come out.

_____ A hard shell called a chrysalis or cocoon is formed.

_____ The female butterfly lays her eggs on a plant.

_____ The caterpillar's skin splits to allow it to crawl out.

_____ The caterpillar eats constantly.

_____ The butterfly is now ready to fly.

_____ After 10 to 14 days, the cocoon suddenly bursts open.

_____ The caterpillar's skin molts one final time, leaving the pupa.

_____ Fluid expands the butterfly's wings, which then dry and harden.

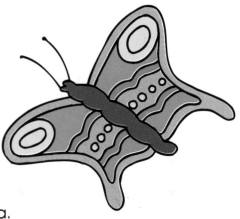

Name: _____

How Do They Relate?

Directions: Circle the correct word to fill in the missing part of each analogy. One is done for you.

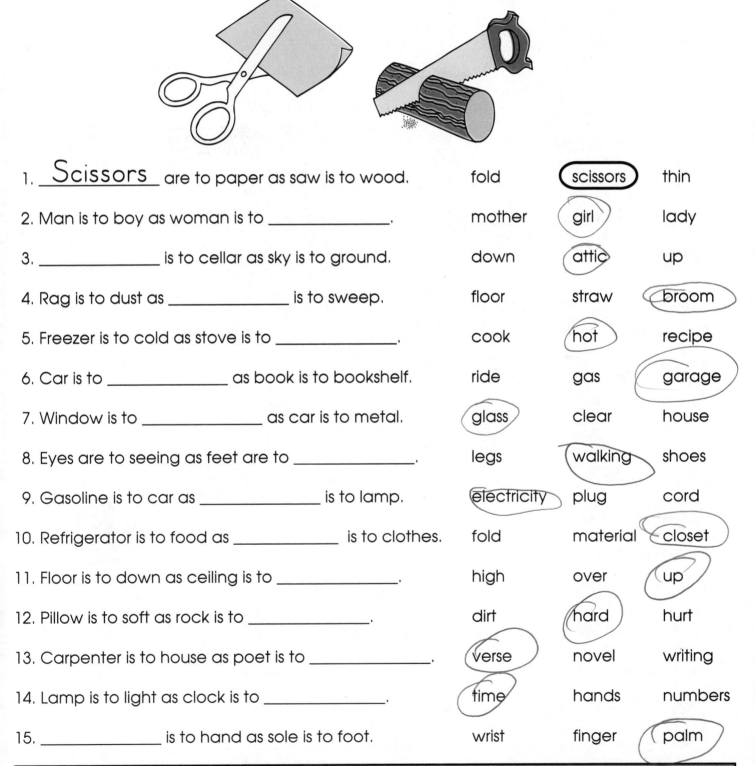

1. __Scissors__ are to paper as saw is to wood.   fold   (scissors)   thin

2. Man is to boy as woman is to _____.   mother   (girl)   lady

3. _____ is to cellar as sky is to ground.   down   (attic)   up

4. Rag is to dust as _____ is to sweep.   floor   straw   (broom)

5. Freezer is to cold as stove is to _____.   cook   (hot)   recipe

6. Car is to _____ as book is to bookshelf.   ride   gas   (garage)

7. Window is to _____ as car is to metal.   (glass)   clear   house

8. Eyes are to seeing as feet are to _____.   legs   (walking)   shoes

9. Gasoline is to car as _____ is to lamp.   (electricity)   plug   cord

10. Refrigerator is to food as _____ is to clothes.   fold   material   (closet)

11. Floor is to down as ceiling is to _____.   high   over   (up)

12. Pillow is to soft as rock is to _____.   dirt   (hard)   hurt

13. Carpenter is to house as poet is to _____.   (verse)   novel   writing

14. Lamp is to light as clock is to _____.   (time)   hands   numbers

15. _____ is to hand as sole is to foot.   wrist   finger   (palm)

More Analogies

Directions: Fill in the blanks with words of your own to complete each analogy. One is done for you.

1. Fuse is to firecracker as wick is to _____candle_____ .

2. Wheel is to steering as _____ is to stopping.

3. Scissors are to _____ as needle is to sew.

4. Water is to skiing as rink is to _____ .

5. Steam shovel is to dig as tractor is to _____.

6. Puck is to hockey as_____ is to baseball.

7. Watch is to television as _____ is to radio.

8. _____ is to goose as children is to child.

9. Multiply is to multiplication as _____ is to subtraction.

10. Milk is to _____ as egg is to _____.

11. Yellow is to banana as _____ is to tomato.

12. _____ is to slow as day is to night.

13. Pine is to tree as _____ is to flower.

14. Zipper is to jacket as _____ is to shirt.

15. Museum is to painting as library is to _____.

16. Petal is to _____ as branch is to _____ .

17. Cow is to barn as _____ is to _____ .

18. _____ is to bedroom as _____ is to kitchen.

19. Teacher is to _____ as _____ is to patient.

20. Ice is to cold as _____ is to _____ .

Name: _____

Fact Or Opinion?

Directions: Read the following sentences about states. Beside each one, write whether it is a fact or opinion. One is done for you.

fact 1. Hawaii is the only island state.

_____ 2. The best fishing is in Michigan.

_____ 3. It is easy to find a job in Wyoming.

_____ 4. Trenton is the capital of New Jersey.

_____ 5. Kentucky is nicknamed the Bluegrass State.

_____ 6. The friendliest people in the United States live in Georgia.

_____ 7. The cleanest beaches are in California.

_____ 8. Summers are most beautiful in Arizona.

_____ 9. Only one percent of North Dakota is forest or woodland.

_____ 10. New Mexico produces almost half of the nation's uranium.

_____ 11. The first shots of the Civil War were fired in South Carolina on April 12, 1861.

_____ 12. The varied geographical features of Washington include moutains, desert, a rain forest, and a volcano.

_____ 13. In 1959, Alaska and Hawaii became the 49th and 50th states to be admitted to the Union.

_____ 14. Wyandotte Cave, one of the largest caves in the United States, is in Indiana.

Directions: Write one fact and one opinion about your own state.

Fact:

_____

Opinion:

_____

_____

23

Name: _____

Fact Or Opinion?

Directions: Read the following very different views of cats. List the facts and opinions in each one.

Cats make the best pets. Domestic or house cats were originally produced by cross-breeding several varieties of wild cats. They were used in ancient Egypt to catch rats and mice, which were overrunning bins of stored grain. Today they are still the most useful domestic animal.

Facts:

1. _____

2. _____

Opinions:

1. _____

2. _____

It is bad luck for a black cat to cross your path. This is one of the many legends about cats. In ancient Egypt, for example, cats were considered sacred, and often were buried with their masters. But during the Middle Ages, cats often were killed for taking part in what people thought were evil deeds. Cats have been thought to bring misfortune.

Facts:

1. _____

2. _____

3. _____

Opinions:

1. _____

2. _____

Name: _____

Causes And Their Effects

Directions: Read the following paragraphs. Complete the charts by writing the missing cause (reason) or effect (result).

Club-footed toads are small toads that live in the rain forests of Central and South America. Because they give off a poisonous substance on their skins, other animals cannot eat them.

Cause:

They give off a poisonous substance.

Effect:

_____

Civets (say it SIV-it) are weasel-like animals. The best-known of the civets is the mongoose, which eats rats and snakes. For this reason, it is welcome around homes in its native India.

Cause:

_____

Effect:

It is welcome around homes in its native India.

Bluebirds can be found in most areas of the United States. Like other members of the thrush family of birds, young bluebirds have speckled breasts. This makes them difficult to see and helps hide them from their enemies. The Pilgrims called them "blue robins" because they are much like the English robin: They are the same size and have the same red breast and friendly song as the English robin.

Cause:

Young bluebirds have speckled breasts.

Effect:

_____

_____

The Pilgrims called them "blue robins."

Name: _____

Review

Directions: Follow the directions for each section.

Cross out the word that does not belong. Add a word of your own that does belong.

1. oak   ~~wood~~   maple   pine   _evergreen_

2. roots   stem   petal   ~~dirt~~   _bulb_

3. ~~paragraph~~   book   newspaper   magazine   _dictionary_

Circle the word that completes each analogy.

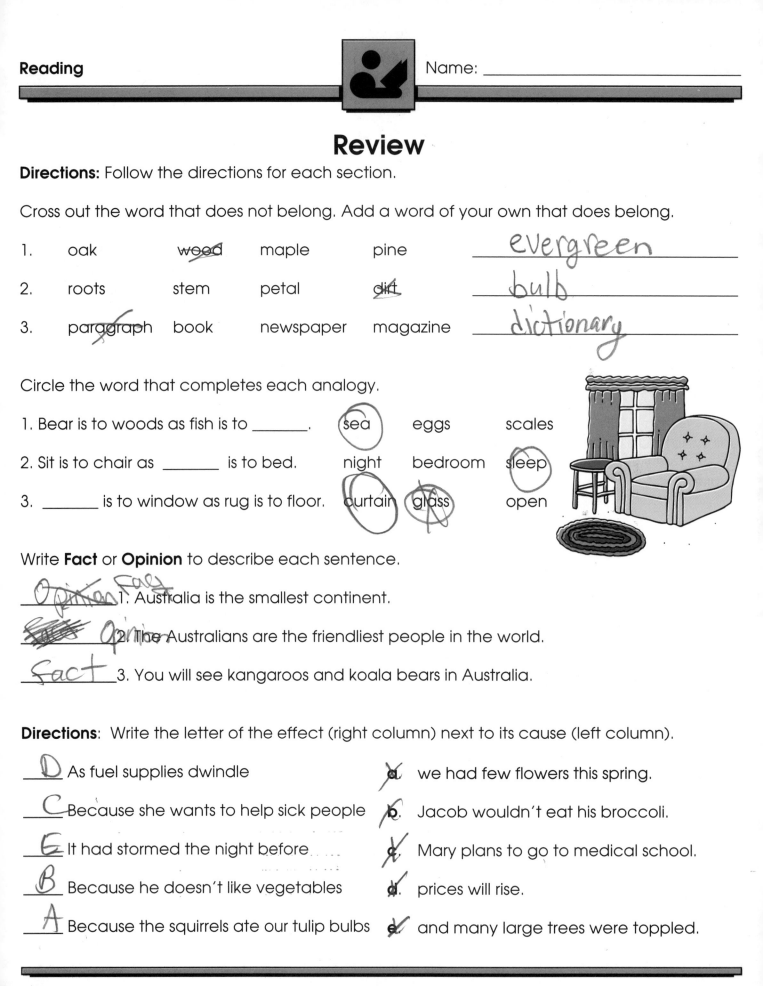

1. Bear is to woods as fish is to _____.   (sea)   eggs   scales

2. Sit is to chair as _____ is to bed.   night   bedroom   (sleep)

3. _____ is to window as rug is to floor.   (curtain)   (glass)   open

Write **Fact** or **Opinion** to describe each sentence.

~~Opinion~~ Fact 1. Australia is the smallest continent.

_~~_____~~ Opinion_ 2. The Australians are the friendliest people in the world.

Fact 3. You will see kangaroos and koala bears in Australia.

Directions: Write the letter of the effect (right column) next to its cause (left column).

_D_ As fuel supplies dwindle   ~~a~~ we had few flowers this spring.

_C_ Because she wants to help sick people   ~~b~~ Jacob wouldn't eat his broccoli.

_E_ It had stormed the night before   ~~c~~ Mary plans to go to medical school.

_B_ Because he doesn't like vegetables   ~~d~~ prices will rise.

_A_ Because the squirrels ate our tulip bulbs ~~e~~ and many large trees were toppled.

Name: _____

Using A Newspaper Index

Newspapers give you all kinds of information. They will tell you about the national and local news, the weather, and sports. You will also find opinions, feature stories, advice columns, comics, entertainment, recipes, advertisements, and more. An index of the newspaper usually appears on the front page.

Directions: Use the newspaper index to answer the following questions. Give the section where you would look and the page numbers where it appears.

Business 8	Local News........5-7
Classified Ads 18-19	National News .. 1-4
Comics 20	Radio-TV 17
Editorials 9	Sports 11-13
Entertainment 14-16	Weather............10

1. Where would you look for results of last night's basketball games?

Sports 11-13

2. Where would you find your favorite cartoon strip? _Comics 20_

3. Where would you find the editor's opinion of upcoming elections?

~~Business~~ Editorials 9

4. Where would you look to locate a used bicycle to buy? _Classified Ads 18-19_

5. Where would you find out if you need to wear your raincoat tomorrow?

Weather 10

6. Where would you find the listing of tonight's TV shows? _Radio-TV 17_

7. Explain which would be first, a story about the President's trip to Europe or a review of the movie "Teenage Mutant Ninja Turtles".

_____

_____

Name: _____

Classified Ads

An advertisement tells about a product or service for sale.

Directions: Read the following advertisements, then answer the questions.

2.

1.

**Yard Work
Breaking Your Back?**
Give Mike and Jane a Crack
Mowing, raking, trash hauled.
References provided.
Call 572-9581

Pet Sitter
Going on vacation?
Away for the weekend?
I am 14 years old and
have experience
caring for dogs and cats.
Your home or mine.
Excellent references.
Call Sally Trent
Phone: 999-8250

3.

**Singing Lessons
for All Ages!**
Be popular at parties!
Fulfill your dreams!
20 years coaching
experience.
Madame Rinaud ...
Coach to the Stars!
787-5331

1. What is promised from the third ad? Is it fact or opinion?

_____

2. What fact is offered in the third ad?

_____

3. Give an example of a slogan, or easy-to-remember phrase, that appears in one of the
   ads.

_____

4. Which ad gives the most facts?

_____

5. Which ad is based mostly on opinion?

_____

Name: _____

What's On TV?

Directions: Use the newspaper program listing below to answer the questions.

Evening

6:00 3 **Let's Talk!** Guest: Animal expert Jim Porter.
        5 **Cartoons**
        8 **News**
        9 **News**

7:00 3 **Farm Report**
        5 **Movie. "A Laugh a Minute"** (1955) James Rayburn.
           Comedy about a boy who wants to join the circus.
        8 **Spin for Dollars**!
        9 **Cooking with Cathy**. Tonight: Chicken with mushrooms.

7:30 3 **Double Trouble** (comedy). The twins disrupt the high
           school dance.
        8 **Wall Street Today**: Stock Market Report

8:00 3 **NBA Basketball**. Teams to be announced
        8 **News Special. "Saving Our Waterways:**
           Pollution in the Mississippi."
        9 **Movie. "At Day's End"** (1981) Michael Collier,
           Julie Romer. Drama set in World War II.

1. What two stations have the news at 6:00?

_____

2. What time would you turn on the television to watch a funny movie? What channel?

_____

3. What might you turn on if you are a sports fan? What time and channel?

_____

4. Which show title sounds like it could be a game show?

_____

5. 1) What show might you want to watch if you are interested in helping the environment?

_____

   2) What time and channel?

_____

Name: _____

Medicine Labels

Directions: Read the label from
a medicine bottle, then answer the questions.

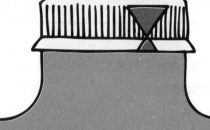

CHILDREN'S
Cough Syrup

Dosages:
Children 2 to 5: 1 teaspoonful
Children 6 to 11: 2 teaspoonfuls
Children Over 12 and Adults:
   4 teaspoonfuls

Repeat every 4 hours as needed. Do not
exceed 8 doses in 24 hours. For children
under 2, consult physician.

Warnings: Do not take this product for
problems related to asthma unless
directed by physician. For coughs lasting
more than a week, or coughs accompanied by fever or rash, consult physician.

> **Remember:** Children should
> never take medicines without
> their parents' knowledge.

1. What is dosage, or amount to be
   taken, for a child three years old?

   _____

2. How often can you take this
   medicine if it is needed?

   _____

3. How many times a day can you
   take this medicine?

4. What should you do before taking the
   medicine if you have a rash in addition
   to your cough?

5. Will this medicine help you if you are
   sneezing?

Name: _____

Reading A Map

Maps give you information about places. Good maps include such features as a legend, compass, scale of distance, latitude/longitude lines, and color key. If you understand them, you can use and understand any map.

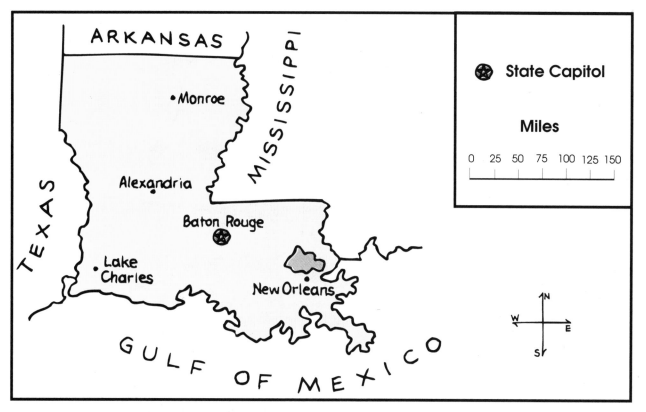

Directions: Use the map to answer the questions.

1. What state borders Louisiana to the north?

_____

2. What is the state capital of Louisiana?

_____

3. What city is located on the Gulf of Mexico?

_____

4. In which direction would you be traveling if you drove from Monroe to Alexandria?

_____

5. About how far is it from Alexandria to Lake Charles?

_____

6. Besides Arkansas, name at least one state that borders Louisiana.

_____

Name: _____

Reading A Map

Directions: Use the map of Columbus, Ohio, to answer the questions.

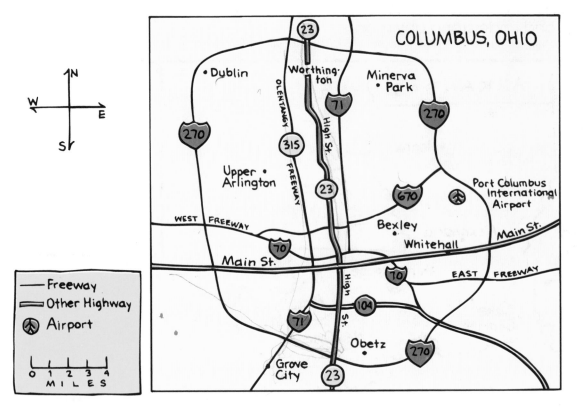

1. Does Highway 104 run east and west or north and south? ___east and west___

2. What is the name of the freeway numbered 315?___OLENTANGY freeway___

3. Which is further south, Bexley or Whitehall? ___whitehall___

4. What two freeways intersect (or cross) near the Port Columbus International Airport?
___270 and 670___

5. Which two cities are farther apart, Dublin and Upper Arlington or Dublin and Worthington?
___Dublin and Upper Arlington___

6. In which direction would you be traveling if you drove from Grove City to Worthington?
___Northwest___

32

Name: _____

Skimming And Scanning

In skimming, look for headings and key words to give you an overall idea of what you are reading.

One of the Earth's Marvels

In America, there is a lot of magnificent scenery. But perhaps the most stunning sight of all is the Grand Canyon. This canyon is in northern Arizona. It is the deepest, widest canyon in the world. It is 217 miles long, 4 to18 miles wide, and, in some places, more than a mile deep. The rocks at the bottom of the steep walls are at least 500 million years old. Most of the rocks are sandstone, limestone, and shale. Because these are water-made rocks, they tell that this part of the world was once under the sea.

Directions: Quickly skim the paragraph to answer this question.

1. What is the "marvel" the paragraph is about?

_____

Directions: Now scan the paragraph to find the answers to the following questions. When scanning, read the questions first, then look for specific words that will help you locate the answers. For example, for the first question, scan for the word "deep."

2. How deep are the lowest points in the Grand Canyon? _____

3. How old are the rocks at the bottom of the Grand Canyon?

_____

4. What kinds of rocks would you find in the Grand Canyon?

_____

5. What do these rocks tell us?

_____

Name: _____

Review

Road Closing Announced

Beginning Monday, drivers in northern Columbus may be facing more traffic jams. The Ohio Department of Transportation has announced that State Route 315 will be closed between Interstates 270 and 670 for repairs. The closing will be in effect for the next three weeks. For alternate routes, drivers can use State Route 23 or Interstate 71.

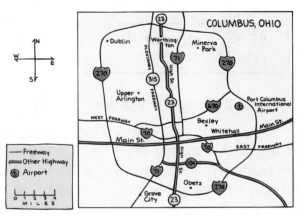

Directions: Skim the paragraph to answer the first question.

1. What announcement is reported in the article?

_____

Directions: Scan the article to answer the following questions.

2. What is the number of the highway that will be closed? _____

3. How long will the road closing be in effect?_____

4. Find the area of the road closing on the map and circle it. _____

5. Using the index, in what section of the paper and on what pages would you find this story?

_____

Business	8	Local News	5-7
Classified Ads	... 18-19	National News	.. 1-4
Editorials	9	Sports	 11-13
Entertainment	.. 14-16	Weather	10

Directions: Read the newspaper advertisement, then answer the questions.

6. What facts are offered in the ad?

_____

_____

7. What opinion is offered in the ad?

_____

_____

> ### Newspaper Carriers Wanted
> Want to earn money? Like having your afternoons free?
> If so, then a newspaper route is for you.
> With a neighborhood route, you can earn money, win prizes, and have a paid vacation!
> If you are at least 12 years of age, call 555-0011
> for more information on this opportunity.

Name: _____

The Coldest Continent

Antarctica

Antarctica, which lies on the South Pole, is the coldest continent. It is without sunlight for months at a time. Even when the sun does shine there, its angle is so slanted that the land receives little warmth. Temperatures often drop to 100 degrees below zero, and a fierce wind blows almost endlessly. Most of the land is covered by snow heaped thousands of feet deep. The snow is so heavy and tightly packed that it forms a great ice cap covering more than 95 percent of the continent.

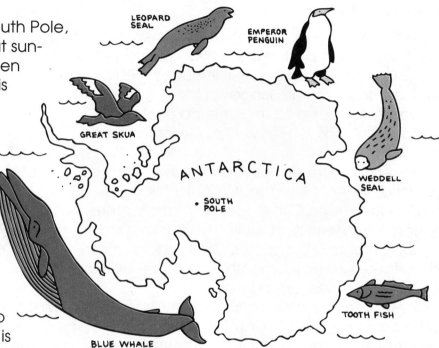

It is no wonder that there are no towns or cities in Antarctica. There is no permanent population at all, only small scientific research stations. Many teams of explorers and scientists have braved the freezing cold since Antarctica was first spotted in 1820. Some have died in their efforts, but a great deal of information has been learned about the continent.

From fossils, pieces of coal, and bone samples, we know that Antarctica was not always an ice-covered land. Scientists believe that 200 million years ago it was connected to southern Africa, South America, Australia, and India. Forests grew in warm swamps, and insects and reptiles thrived there. Today, there are animals that live in and around the waters that border the continent. In fact, the waters surrounding Antarctica hold more life than oceans in warmer areas of the world.

Directions: Answer these questions about Antarctica.

1. Where is Antarctica? _____

2. How much of the continent is covered by an ice cap? _____

3. When was Antarctica first sighted by explorers? _____

4. What things have provided clues that Antarctica was not always an ice-covered land?

_____

Name: _____

The Other Pole

The Arctic Circle

On the other side of the world from Antarctica, at the northernmost part of the world, is another icy land. This is the Arctic Circle. It includes the North Pole itself, the northern fringes of three continents — Europe, Asia, and North America (including the state of Alaska) — as well as Greenland and other islands.

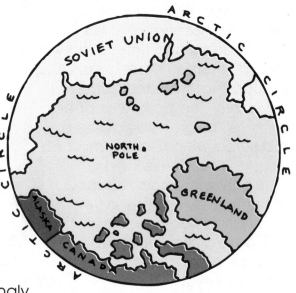

The seasons are opposite on the two ends of the world. When it is summer in Antarctica, it is winter in the Arctic Circle. In both places, there are very long periods of sunlight in summer and very long nights in the winter. On the poles themselves, there are six full months of sunlight and six full months of darkness each year.

Compared to Antarctica, the summers are surprisingly mild in some areas of the Arctic Circle. Much of the snow cover may melt, and temperatures often reach 50 degrees in July. But neither of the polar regions can support plant life. Antarctica is covered by water — frozen water, of course — so nothing can grow there. Plant growth is limited in the polar regions not only by the cold, but also by wind, lack of water, and the long winter darkness.

In the Far North, willow trees do grow, but only to be a few inches high! The annual rings — the circles within the trunk of a tree that show its age and how fast it grows — in these trees are so narrow that you need a microscope to see them.

A permanently frozen layer of soil, called "permafrost," keeps roots from growing deep enough into the ground to anchor a plant. Even if a plant could survive the cold temperatures, it could not grow roots deep enough or strong enough to allow the plant to get very big.

Directions: Answer these questions about the Arctic Circle.

1. What three continents have land included in the Arctic Circle?

a._____ b._____ c._____

2. Is the Arctic Circle generally warmer or colder than Antarctica?_____

3. What are the annual rings of a tree? _____

4. What is "permafrost"? _____

Name: _____

Blazing The Polar Trail

Antarctica, the last continent to be discovered, was not sighted until the early nineteenth century. Since then, many brave explorers and adventurers have sailed south to conquer the icy land. Their achievements once gained as much attention as those of the first astronauts.

Long before the continent was first spotted, the ancient Greeks had guessed that there was a continent at the bottom of the world. Over the centuries, legends of the undiscovered land spread. Some of the world's greatest seamen tried to find it, including Captain James Cook in 1772.

Cook was the first to sail all the way to the solid field of ice that surrounds Antarctica every winter. In fact, he sailed all the way around the continent but never saw it. Cook went farther south than anyone had ever gone. His record lasted fifty years.

Forty years after Cook, a new kind of seaman sailed the icy waters. They were the hunters of seals and whales. Sailing through unknown waters in search of seals, these men became explorers as well as hunters. It is believed that the first person to sight Antarctica was one of these hunters, a 21-year-old American named Nathaniel Brown Palmer. The year was 1820.

Directions: Answer these questions about Antarctica.

Check √

1. The main idea is:

☐ Antarctica was not sighted until the early nineteenth century.

☐ Many brave explorers and adventurers have sailed south to conquer the icy land.

Write

2. Who was the first person to sail to the ice field that surrounds Antarctica?

_____

3. How long did his record for sailing the farthest south stand? _____

4. Who is thought to be the first man to sight Antarctica? _____

5. What was his profession? _____

37

Exploring The Frozen Continent

By the mid-1800s, most of the seals of Antarctica had been killed off. The seal hunters no longer sailed the icy waters. The explorers who next took an interest in Antarctica were scientists. Of these, one who took the most daring chances and made the most amazing discoveries was British Captain James Clark Ross.

Ross first made a name for himself sailing to the north. In 1831, he discovered the North Magnetic Pole — one of two places on earth toward which a compass needle points. In 1840, Ross set out to find the South Magnetic Pole. He made many marvelous discoveries, including the Ross Sea, a great open sea beyond the ice packs that stopped other explorers, and the Ross Ice Shelf, a great floating sheet of ice bigger than all of France!

The next man to make his mark exploring Antarctica was the British explorer Robert Falcon Scott. Scott set out in 1902 to find the South Pole. He and his team suffered greatly, but they were able to make it a third of the way to the pole. Back in England, Scott was a great hero. In1910, he again attempted to become the first man to reach the South Pole. But this time he had competition: An explorer from Norway, Roald Amundsen, was also leading a team to the South Pole.

It was a brutal race. Both teams faced many hardships, but they pressed on. Finally, on December 14, 1911, Amundsen became the first man ever to reach the South Pole. Scott arrived on January 17, 1912. He was bitterly disappointed at not being first. The trip back was even more horrible. Not one of the five men in the Scott expedition survived.

Directions: Answer these questions about explorers.

1. After the seal hunters, who were the next group of explorers interested in Antarctica?

_____

2. Name two of the great discoveries made by James Ross.

1) _____   2)_____

3. What big discovery did James Ross make before ever sailing to Antarctica?

_____

4. How close did Scott and his team come to finding the South Pole in 1902?

_____

5. Who was the first man to reach the South Pole? _____

Name: _____

Polar Bears

There are animals that are able to survive the cold weather and difficult conditions of the snow and ice fields in the polar regions. One of the best known is the polar bear of the North Pole.

Polar bears live on the land and the sea. They may drift hundreds of miles from land on huge sheets of floating ice. They use their great paws to paddle the ice along. Polar bears are excellent swimmers, too. They can cross great distances of open water. While in the sea, they feed mostly on fish and seals.

On the land, these huge animals, which measure ten feet long and weigh about 1000 pounds, can run 25 miles an hour. Surprisingly, polar bears live as plant eaters rather than hunters while on land. Unlike many kinds of bears, polar bears do not hibernate. They are active the whole year long.

Baby polar bears are born during the winter. They are pink and almost hairless. These helpless cubs weigh only two pounds — less than one-third the size of most human infants. The mother rears her young in dens dug in snow banks. By the time they are ten weeks old, polar bear cubs are about the size of puppies and have enough white fur to protect them in the open air. The mother gives her cubs swimming, hunting, and fishing lessons. But by the time autumn comes, the cubs are left to survive on their own.

Directions: Answer these questions about polar bears.

Circle **Yes** or **No**

1. Polar Bears can live on the land and on the sea.   Yes   No

2. Polar Bears are excellent swimmers.   Yes   No

3. Polar Bears hibernate in the winter.   Yes   No

4. A newborn polar bear weighs more than a newborn human baby.   Yes   No

5. Mother polar bears raise their babies in caves.   Yes   No

6. Father bears give the cubs swimming lessons.   Yes   No

Name: _____

Seals

Seals are **aquatic** mammals that have kept a liking for land. Some seals stay in the sea for weeks or months at a time, even sleeping in the water. But all seals need the land at some time. To avoid people and other animals, they pick **secluded** spots to come onto the land.

The 31 different kinds of seals belong to a group of animals that is often called "pinnipeds", or fin-footed. Their fins, or flippers, make them very good swimmers and divers. Their nostrils close tightly when they dive. They have been known to stay **submerged** for as long as a half-hour at a time!

Seals are warm-blooded animals that can adjust to various temperatures. They live in both **temperate** and cold climates. Besides their fur, seals have a thick layer of fat called "blubber" to help protect them against the cold. It is harder for seals to cool themselves in hot weather than to warm themselves in cold weather. They sometimes can become so overheated that they die.

Directions: Answer these questions about seals.

Check √

1. Based on the other words in the sentence, what is the correct definition for "aquatic"?
   - ☐ living on the land
   - ☐ living on or in the sea
   - ☐ living in large groups

2. Based on the other words in the sentence, what is the correct definition for "secluded"?
   - ☐ rocky
   - ☐ private or hidden
   - ☐ near other animals

3. Based on the other words in the sentence, what is the correct definition for "submerged"?
   - ☐ under the water
   - ☐ on top of the water
   - ☐ in groups

4. Based on the other words in the sentence, what is the correct definition for "temperate"?
   - ☐ rainy
   - ☐ measured on a thermometer
   - ☐ warm

The Walrus

   Walruses are actually a kind of seal that live only in the Arctic Circle. They have two huge upper teeth, or tusks, they use to pull themselves out of the water or to move over the rocks on land. They also use them to dig clams, one of their favorite foods, from the bottom of the sea. In an adult male walrus, the tusks may be three and a half feet long!

   Walruses have unusual faces. Besides their long tusks, they have big, bushy mustaches made up of hundreds of movable, stiff bristles. They help the walrus to push food into his mouth. Also, except for a small wrinkle in the skin, walruses have no outer ears.

   Like the seal, the walrus uses his flippers to help him swim. His front flippers serve as paddles, and he swings the back of his huge body from side to side. A walrus looks awkward using his flippers to walk on land, but don't be fooled! A walrus can run as fast as a man.

   Baby walruses are born in the early spring. They never leave their mothers until they are two years old. There is a good reason for this — they must grow little tusks, at least three or four inches long, before they can catch their own food from the bottom of the sea. Until then, they must stay close to their mothers to eat. A young walrus that is tired from swimming will climb onto his mother's back for a ride, holding onto her with his front flippers.

Directions: Answers these questions about walruses.

1. The walrus is a type of seal found only _____.

2. List two ways the walrus uses his tusks.

   1) _____

   2) _____

Directions: Circle **Yes** or **No**

3. A walrus cannot move quickly on land.   Yes   No

4. A baby walrus must stay very close to its mother until it is two years old.   Yes   No

Name: _____

Review

Penguins are among the best-liked animals in the world. People are amused by their funny duck-like waddle and their appearance of wearing little tuxedos. But the penguin is a much misunderstood animal. There may be more wrong ideas about penguins than any other animal.

For example, many people are surprised to learn that penguins are really birds. Penguins do not fly, but they do have feathers, and only birds have feathers. Also, like other birds, penguins build nests and their young are hatched from eggs. Because of their unusual looks, though, you would never confuse them with any other bird!

Penguins are also thought of as symbols of the polar regions. But no penguins have ever lived north of the equator, so you would not find a penguin on the North Pole. Penguins don't live at the South Pole, either. Just two of the seventeen **species** of penguin spend all of their lives on the frozen continent of Antarctica. You would be just as likely to see a penguin living on an island in a warm climate as in a cold area.

Directions: Answer these questions about penguins.

Check √

1. The main idea is:
   - ☐ Penguins are among the best-liked animals in the world.
   - ☐ The penguin is a much misunderstood animal.

2. Penguins live
   - ☐ only at the North Pole
   - ☐ only at the South Pole
   - ☐ only south of the equator

3. Based on the other words in the sentence, what is the correct definition of the word "species"?
   - ☐ number
   - ☐ bird
   - ☐ a distinct kind

Write

4. List three ways penguins are like other birds.

   1) _____

   2) _____

   3) _____

The Earliest Forms Of Printing

When people talk about printing, they usually mean making exact copies of an original document, such as a paper or even an entire book. The inventions that have allowed us to do this are some of the most important developments in the history of man. Look around you. How many examples can you find of things that have been printed? Can you imagine life without it?

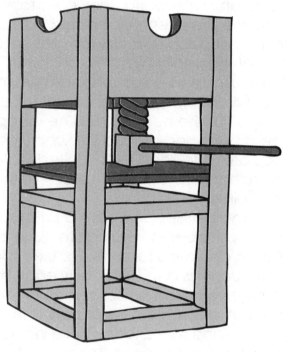

The oldest known example of a printed book was made in China in 848. A man named Wang Chieh made the book by carving each page by hand onto a block of wood. He then put ink on the wood and pressed it to a piece of paper. This idea of printing with wood blocks spread to Europe. The letters in these block books were made to look handwritten.

In about 1440, a German goldsmith named Johann Gutenberg developed the idea of movable type. This meant that letters were made separately. The letters could be fastened together to make words and sentences. They were made out of metal so they could be used again and again. This wonderful invention made it possible to have more and cheaper reading material.

Gutenberg had other ideas that were important to printing. He developed a kind of ink that would stick to the new metal type. Gutenberg's ideas were so successful that the process of printing went almost unchanged for more than 300 years.

Directions: Answer these questions about printing.

1. In what country was the oldest known printed book made?_____

2. What is "movable type"?_____

3. What was the name of the man who developed the idea of movable type?

_____

4. What was another important invention of Gutenberg? _____

5. Who made the first printed book? _____

Name: _____

Read All About It!

Newspapers. They keep us informed about what is going on in the world. They entertain, educate, and examine the events of the day. For hundreds of millions of people worldwide, newspapers are part of their daily lives.

Newspapers are published at various intervals, but they usually come out daily or weekly. Of the nearly 60,000 newspapers being published around the world, about 2600 are published in the United States. More than half — about 1800 — of them are dailies.

Some newspapers have a lot of sub-scribers — people who pay to have each edition delivered to them. For example, *The Wall Street Journal* and *USA Today* each have about two million subscribers. But there are many, many more newspapers with only a few thosand subscribers. These include small-town weeklies and special-interest papers, such as those written for people who enjoy the same hobby.

Newspapers provide a service to the community by providing information at little cost. But they are businesses, so they need to make money. They can keep the cost to the reader low and still stay in business by selling space to businesses and individuals who want to advertise products or services. In most newspapers, between one-third and two-thirds of the paper is taken up by advertising.

Directions: Answer these questions about newspapers.

1. How many newspapers are thought to be published worldwide?_____

2. What are "subscribers"?_____

3. At what intervals are most newspapers published?_____

4. What do newspapers do to keep the cost to the reader low but still make money?

_____

Name: _____

The First Newspapers

The earliest newspapers were probably handwritten notices posted to be read by the public. But the first true newspaper was a weekly newspaper started in Germany in 1609. It was called the *Strassburg Relation*. The Germans were pioneers in newspaper publishing. (Johann Gutenberg, the man who developed the idea of movable type, was from Germany.)

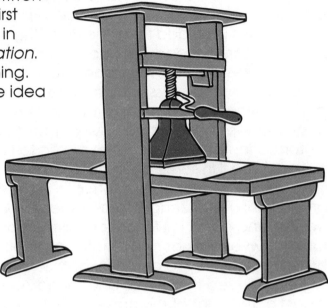

One of the first English-language newspapers, *The London Gazette*, was printed in England in 1665. "Gazette" is an old English word that means "official publication". Many newspapers today still use the word gazette in their names.

In America, several papers were started during the colonial days. The first successful one, *The Boston News-Letter,* began printing in 1704.

It was very small — about the size of a sheet of notebook paper with printing on both sides.

An important date in newspaper publishing was 1833. In that year, *The New York Sun* became the first penny newspaper. They actually did cost only a penny. The penny newspapers were similar to today's papers: they printed news while it was still new, they were the first to print advertisements and to sell papers in newsstands, and penny newspapers were the first to be delivered to homes.

Directions: Answer these questions about early newspapers.

1. In what year was the first true newspaper printed?_____

2. What was the name of the first successful newspaper in America?

_____

3. Why was 1833 important in newspaper publishing?_____

4. List four ways the penny newspapers were like the newspapers of today.

1) _____   3) _____

2) _____   4) _____

Name: _____

Freedom Of The Press

In the United States, we have certain rights or freedoms that are **guaranteed** to us by the Constitution. Freedom of the press is one of the **privileges** provided for in the Bill of Rights. Press originally referred to newspapers, magazines, books, pamphlets — anything printed on a printing press. Today, television, movies, and radio are also included.

Freedom of the press is the right to gather and publish information or opinions without the control of the government. Before the Bill of Rights, the government could stop newspapers from writing stories it didn't like or information it didn't want the public to know. This form of **censorship** is still practiced in some countries.

An important test of freedom of the press occurred in 1735. A man named John Peter Zenger, a newspaper publisher in New York, was arrested and put in jail for **criticizing** the colonial government. At his trial, his lawyer did not deny that Zenger printed the material. But he challenged the jury to decide whether what Zenger printed was true. The jury believed that it was and found Zenger not guilty. This was the first test of the right of the press to print the truth, even if the government didn't like it.

Directions: Answer these questions about freedom of the press.

Check √

1. Based on the other words in the sentence, what is the correct definition for "guaranteed"?
   - ☐ written
   - ☐ pledged or promised
   - ☐ provide

2. Based on the other words in the sentence, what is the correct definition for "privilege"?
   - ☐ right
   - ☐ law
   - ☐ anything printed

3. Based on the other words in the sentence, what is the correct definition for "censorship"?
   - ☐ laws
   - ☐ writing
   - ☐ not allowing certain information to be published

4. Based on the other words in the sentence, what is the correct definition for "criticizing"?
   - ☐ disapproving of
   - ☐ agreeing with
   - ☐ talking about

Jobs At A Newspaper

It takes a whole army of people to put out one of the big daily newspapers. There are three separate departments needed to make a newspaper operate smoothly: editorial, mechanical, and business.

The editorial department is the one most people think about first. That is the news-gathering part of the newspaper. The most familiar job in this department is that of the reporter — the person who gets the information for a story and writes it. A photographer takes the pictures to go with the reporter's story.

Editors are the decision makers. There are many editors at a newspaper to do such jobs as assigning the stories to reporters, reading the stories to make sure they are correct, and deciding where the stories should appear in the paper. The most important stories go on the front page. There are also picture editors who choose which pictures will appear in the paper. Other jobs in the editorial department include artists, copy editors, proofreaders, and cartoonists.

The biggest job in the mechanical department is printing the paper. Most larger news-papers have their own printing presses. Some small papers send their work to outside printing shops. After an issue, or edition, is printed, it is ready to be sold or "circulated" to the public.

The circulation of the paper is one of the jobs of the business department. This depart-ment also sells the advertising space. This is very important for newspapers. Many papers make more money selling advertising space than selling newspapers. The business depart-ment also takes care of normal business jobs, such as paying the bills and keeping records.

Directions: Answer these questions about newspaper jobs.

1. Name the three main departments at a newspaper.

1)_____ 2)_____ 3)_____

2. Who are the people who get the information for a story and write it? _____

3. Who are the decision-makers at a newspaper?_____

4. What is the biggest job for the mechanical department?_____

Name: _____

The Story Of A Story

Here is an example of how a story gets into the newspaper:

Let's imagine that a city bus has turned over in a ditch, injuring some of the passengers. An **eyewitness** calls the newspaper. The editor assigns a reporter to go to the scene. The reporter talks to the passengers. She finds out what they saw and how they feel, writing down their comments in a notebook. At the same time, a photographer is busy taking pictures.

If there isn't time for the reporter to go back to the office, she telephones it in. A copytaker types the story onto a computer as the reporter **dictates** it. (Many newspapers today have word processors on which the reporter can write the story on the spot, and then send it back to the office over the telephone lines.) Next an editor will read the story, checking the facts and making sure there are no grammar or spelling mistakes. Meanwhile, the photographer's film is developed and a picture is chosen. It is sent to the processing department.

The story is set in print. On most newspapers today, this can be done with a computer. The computer makes sets of columns of type, which are pasted onto a sheet of paper exactly the same size as a newspaper page. A **proofreader** checks the story for mistakes. The newpaper is now ready for printing. The presses begin to run. Miles of paper are turned into thousands of printed, cut, and folded newspapers. They are counted and put into bundles, and placed in waiting trucks. Within only a few hours, people can read about the bus accident in their daily newspaper.

Directions: Answer these questions about news stories.

Check √

1. Based on the other words in the sentence, what is the correct definition for "eyewitness"?
   - ☐ a reporter
   - ☐ a person who saw what happened
   - ☐ a lawyer

2. Based on the other words in the sentence, what is the correct definition for "dictates"?
   - ☐ photographs
   - ☐ writes
   - ☐ reads story word for word

3. Based on the other words in the sentence, what is the correct definition for "proofreader"?
   - ☐ person who reads for mistakes
   - ☐ teacher
   - ☐ printer

Name: _____

News Services

Most people who read daily newspapers expect to see news from all over the world. Some newspapers do have offices or reporters in Washington, D.C., and other major cities around the world. But most newspapers rely on news services for international news. These are organizations that gather and sell news to papers and even radio and television stations. They are sometimes referred to as "wire services" because they would send stories over telegraph or teletype lines, or "wires."

The two largest news services are the Associated Press and United Press International. Stories sent by these services have their initials — AP or UPI — at the beginning. All large American newspapers are members of either the AP or UPI services.

The gathering of news from around the world has been greatly speeded up by the inventions of the telegraph, telephone, cable, radio, teletype and facsimile machines. Today, stories and even pictures can be sent around the world in a matter of minutes.

Directions: Answer these questions about news services.

1. What is another name for news service organizations? _____

2. List the two largest news service organizations.

1)_____

2)_____

3. List three inventions that have speeded the worldwide gathering of news.

1)_____

2)_____

3)_____

Review

Samuel Langhorne Clemens was born in Florida, Missouri, in 1835. In his lifetime, he gained worldwide fame as a writer, lecturer, and humorist.

Clemens first worked for a printer when he was only 12 years old. Soon after that he worked on his brother's newspaper.

Clemens traveled a lot and worked as a printer in New York, Philadelphia, St. Louis, and Cincinnati. On a trip to New Orleans in 1857, he learned the difficult art of steamboat piloting. Clemens loved this and later used it as a background for some of his books, including *Life on the Mississippi*.

A few years later, Clemens went to Nevada with his brother and tried goldmining. When this proved unsuccessful, he went back to writing for newspapers. At first he signed his humorous pieces with the name "Josh." But in 1863, he began signing them Mark Twain. The words "mark twain" are used by river pilots to mean "two fathoms (12 feet) deep" — safe water for steamboats. From then on, Clemens used this now-famous **pseudonym** for all of his writing.

As Mark Twain, he began to receive attention from all over the world. His best-known works include *Tom Sawyer* and *The Adventures of Huckleberry Finn*. These are still two of the most beloved books about boyhood.

Directions: Answer these questions about Samuel Clemens.

Write

1. Under what name did Samuel Clemens write his books?_____

2. What do the words "mark twain" really mean? _____

3. Besides author, list two other jobs held by Mark Twain.

1) _____ 2)_____

4. List two of the best-known books written by Mark Twain.

1)_____ 2)_____

Check √

5. Based on the other words in the sentence, what is the correct definition for "pseudonym"?
- ☐ book title
- ☐ a made-up name used by an author
- ☐ a humorous article

Name: _____

The Desert

Deserts are found where there is little rainfall, or where the rainfall for a whole year falls in only a few weeks' time. Ten inches of rain may be enough for many plants to survive if the rain is spread out throughout the year. But if the ten inches falls during one or two months and the rest of the year is dry, a desert may form.

When many people think of deserts, they think of long stretches of sand. Sand begins as tiny pieces of rock that get smaller and smaller as wind and weather wear them down. Sand dunes, or hills of drifting sand, are made as winds move the sand over the desert. Grain by grain, the dune grows over the years, always shifting with the winds and changing its shape. Most dunes are only a few feet tall, but they can grow to be several hundred feet high.

There is, however, much more to a desert than sand. In the deserts of the southwestern United States, cliffs and canyons were formed from thick mud that once lay beneath a sea more than a hundred million years ago. Over the centuries, the water drained away. Wind, sand, rain, heat, and cold all carved away at the remaining rocks. The faces of the desert mountains are always changing — very, very slowly — as these forces of nature continue to work on the rock.

Most deserts have surprising varieties of life. There are plants, animals, and insects that have adapted to life in the desert. During the heat of the day, a visitor may see very few signs of living things. But as the air begins to cool in the evening, the desert comes to life. As the sun begins to rise again in the sky, the desert is once again quiet and lonely.

Directions: Answer these questions about deserts.

Circle **Yes** or **No**

1. Deserts are found where there is little rainfall or where
   the rainfall for a whole year falls in only a few weeks.   Yes   No

2. Sand begins as tiny pieces of rock that get smaller and
   smaller as wind and weather wear them down.   Yes   No

3. Sand dunes were formed from thick mud that once lay
   beneath a sea more than a hundred million years ago.   Yes   No

4. The faces of the desert mountains can never change.   Yes   No

5. Most deserts have surprising varieties of life.   Yes   No

Name: _____

Desert Weather

One definition of a desert is an area that has, on the average, less than ten inches of rain a year. Many deserts have far less than that. Death Valley in the United States, for example, receives less than two inches of rain each year. The driest of all is the Atacama Desert in Chile, where no rain at all has ever been known to fall!

Some deserts have a regular rainy season each year, but usually desert rainfall is totally unpredictable. An area may have no rainfall for many years, and then suddenly be flooded by rain. Sometimes a passing cloud may look like it will send relief to the waiting land,

but only a "ghost rain" falls. This means that the hot, dry air dries up the raindrops long before they ever reach the ground.

The temperatures in the desert range greatly. The daytime temperatures in the desert frequently top 120 degrees. In Death Valley, they have been know to reach 190 degrees! In most parts of the world, the moisture in the air works like a blanket to hold the heat of the day close to the earth at night. But, because it has no moisture, the desert has no such blanket. This means that the nighttime temperatures are very chilly. Temperatures have been known to drop fifty or even one hundred degrees at night.

Directions: Answer these questions about desert weather.

1. How much rainfall in a year is used in one definition of desert?_____

2. What is the driest desert in the world? _____

3. What is a "ghost rain"? _____

_____

4. In other parts of the world, what works as a "blanket" to hold the heat of the day close to

the earth at night? _____

5. Are the nights in the deserts hot or cold? _____

Name: _____

Lakes In The Desert?

A few deserts have small permanent lakes. While they may be a welcome sight in the desert, the water in them is not fit for drinking. These lakes are salt lakes. Rains from nearby higher land keep these lakes supplied with water. But, because the lakes are blocked in with nowhere to drain, over the years mineral salts collect there and build up to a high level.

Most desert lakes are only temporary. The occasional rains may fill them to depths of several feet, but in a matter of weeks or months all of the water has been dried up by the heat and sun. The dried lake beds that remain are called playas. Some playas are simply areas of sun-baked mud; others are covered with a sparkling layer of salt.

Perhaps the most unusual desert lake is in central Australia. It is called Lake Eyre. It is a huge lake — nearly 3,600 square miles in area — but it is almost totally dry most of the time. Since it was discovered in 1840, it has been filled only two times. Both times the lake completely dried up within a few years.

Directions: Answer these questions about desert lakes.

1. Why is the water in a desert lake not fit for drinking?_____

2. Why are the lakes in the desert salt lakes? _____

_____

3. What is a "playa"? _____

4. Name the desert lake in central Australia. _____

5. How big is this desert lake? _____

Name: _____

Desert Plants

Desert plants have special features, or adaptations, that allow them to **survive** the harsh conditions of the desert. A cactus stores water in its tissues at times of rain. It then can use this supply over a long dry season. The tiny needles on some kinds of **cacti** may number in the tens of thousands. These sharp thorns protect the cactus. They also form tiny shadows in the sunlight that help keep the plant from getting too hot.

Other plants are able to live by dropping their leaves. This cuts down on the **evaporation** of their water supply in the hot sun. Still other plants survive as seeds, protected from the sun and heat by tough seed coats. When it rains, the seeds **sprout** quickly, bloom, and produce more seeds that can **withstand** long dry spells.

Some plants spread their roots close to the earth's surface to quickly gather water when it does rain. Other plants, such as the mesquite (say it mes-KEET), have roots that grow fifty or sixty feet below the earth's surface to reach underground water supplies.

Directions: Answer these questions about desert plants.

Check √

1. Based on the other words in the sentence, what is the correct definition for "survive"?
   - ☐ continue to live
   - ☐ die
   - ☐ flower

2. Based on the other words in the sentence, what is the correct definition of "cacti"?
   - ☐ kind of leaf
   - ☐ more than one cactus
   - ☐ roots

3. Based on the other words in the sentence, what is the correct definition of "evaporation"?
   - ☐ water loss from heat
   - ☐ increased
   - ☐ boiling

4. Based on the other words in the sentence, what is the correct definition of "sprout"?
   - ☐ die
   - ☐ begin to grow
   - ☐ flower

5. Based on the other words in the sentence, what is the correct definition of "withstand"?
   - ☐ put up with
   - ☐ stand up
   - ☐ take from

The Cactus Family

Cacti are the best-known desert plants. But cacti don't live only in hot, dry places. While they are most likely to be found in the desert areas of Mexico and southwestern United States, they can be seen as far north as Nova Scotia. There are certain types of cactus that can live even in the snow.

Desert cacti are particularly good at surviving very long dry spells. Most cacti have a very good root system so they can absorb as much water as possible. Every available drop of water is taken into the cactus and held in its fleshy stem. A cactus stem can hold enough water to last for two years or longer.

The cactus may be best know for its spines. Although a few kinds of cactus don't have spines, the stems of most types are covered with these sharp needles. The spines have many uses for the cactus. They keep animals from eating the cactus. They collect raindrops and dew. The spines also help keep the plant cool by forming shadows in the sun and by trapping a layer of air close to the plant. They break up the desert winds that dry out the cactus.

Cacti come in all sizes and shapes. The biggest cactus in North America is the saguaro (sa-GWAH-row). It can weigh 12,000 to 14,000 pounds and grow to be fifty feet tall. A saguaro can last several years without water, but it will grow only after summer rains. In May and June, white blossoms appear. Many kinds of birds nest in this enormous cactus: white-winged doves, woodpeckers, small owls, thrashers, and wrens all build nests in the saguaro.

Directions: Answer these questions about cacti.

1. Where are you most likely to find a cactus growing? _____

_____

2. How long can most cacti survive without water?_____

3. What are some ways the cactus uses its spines?_____

_____

4. What is the biggest cactus in North America?_____

Lizards

Lizards are reptiles, so they are cousins to snakes, turtles, alligators and crocodiles. Like other reptiles, lizards are cold-blooded. This means that their body temperatures change with that of their surroundings. However, by changing their behavior throughout the day they can keep their temperature fairly constant.

Usually, the lizard comes out of its burrow early in the morning. Most lizards like to lie in the sun to warm up before starting their daily activities. In the mid-morning, they hunt for food. If it becomes too hot, lizards can raise their tails and bodies off of the ground to help cool off. At mid-day, they return to their burrows or crawl under rocks for several hours. Late in the day, they again lie in the sun to absorb heat before the chilly desert night.

Like all animals, lizards have ways to protect themselves. Some types of lizard have developed a most unusual defense. If a hawk or other animal grabs one of these lizards by its tail, the tail will break off. The tail will continue to wiggle around to distract the attacker while the lizard runs away. A month or two later, the lizard will grow a new tail.

There are abut 3000 kinds of lizards, and all of them can bite. But only two types of lizard are poisonous: the Gila (HE-la) monster of the southwestern United States and the Mexican beaded lizard. Both are short-legged, thick-bodied reptiles with fat tails. These lizards do not attack human beings and will not bite them unless they are being attacked by the human.

Directions: Answer these questions about lizards.

1. What does "cold-blooded" mean? _____

_____

2. What can a lizard do if it becomes too hot? _____

3. What part of the lizard can break off if the animal is caught by an attacker?

_____

4. What two kinds of lizards are poisonous?

1)_____   2)_____

Name: _____

Man In The Desert

Long before the white man came to live in America, Native Americans had discovered ways for living in the desert. Some of these Native Americans were hunters or belonged to wandering tribes that stayed in the desert for only short periods of time. Others learned to farm and live in villages. They made their houses of trees, clay, and brush.

The desert met all of their needs for life: food, skins for clothing, and materials for tools, weapons, and shelter. For meat, the desert offered deer, birds, and rabbits for hunting. When these larger animals were hard to find, the Native Americans would eat mice and lizards. Many desert plants, such as the prickly pear and mesquite, provide fruit and seeds that can be eaten.

The first white men to come to the desert were searching for furs and metals, such as silver and gold. These pioneers were usually unsuccessful at living in the desert. They found the great heat and long dry periods too difficult to live with. When they left, they left behind empty mining camps, houses, and sheds that have slowly fallen apart in the sun and wind.

Directions: Answer these questions about deserts.

Check √
1. The main idea is:
   - ☐ Before the white man came to live in America, Native Americans had discovered ways for living in the desert.
   - ☐ Some Native Americans were hunters or belonged to wandering tribes who stayed in the desert for only short periods of time.

Write
2. Who were the first humans to live in the desert?_____

3. What did the Native Americans use to make their houses in the desert?

_____

4. What kind of food did the Native Americans find in the desert?

_____

5. Who were the white men who came to live in the desert?

_____

Review

Camels are well suited to desert life. They can cope with infrequent supplies of food and water, blazing heat during the day and low temperatures at night, and sand blown by high winds.

There are two kinds of camels: the two-humped Bactrian (BACK-tre-an) and the one-humped dromedary (DROM-a-dare-ee). The dromedary is the larger of the two. It has coarse fur on its back that helps protect it from the sun's rays. The hair on its stomach and legs is short to prevent overheating. When camels **molt** in the spring, their wool can be collected in tufts from the bushes and ground.

The legs of the dromedary are much longer than those of the Bactrian. Animals that live in very hot countries tend to have longer legs. This gives them a larger area of body surface for heat to escape from. Bactrian camels live in the deserts of central Asia where winters are bitterly cold, so they are not as tall as the dromedary.

Both kinds of camel have pads on their feet that keep them from sinking into the sand as they walk across it. The camel's long neck allows it to reach the ground to drink water and eat grass without having to bend its legs. It also can reach up to eat leaves from the trees.

The camel does not store water in its hump, as many people believe. The hump is a fat storage. When there is plenty of food, the camel's hump swells and feels firm. During the dry season when there is little food, the fat is used up and the hump shrinks and becomes soft.

Directions: Answer these questions about camels.

Check √

1. The main idea is:
   - ☐ Camels are well suited to desert life.
   - ☐ There are two kinds of camels.

2. Based on the other words in the sentence, what is the correct definition for "molt"?
   - ☐ gets sick
   - ☐ sheds its hair
   - ☐ becomes overheated

Write

3. List the two kinds of camels.

1)_____   2)_____

4. Which kind of camel has one hump?_____

5. Why doesn't a camel sink into the sand when it walks?

_____

_____

Name: _____

Railroads

As early as the 1550s, a rough form of railroad was already being used in parts of Europe. Miners in England and other areas of western Europe used horse-drawn wagons on wooden tracks to pull loads out of the mines. With these tracks, the horses could carry twice as much coal as they could without them. But no one could have known that one day this simple idea would change the world.

There were many developments along the way that helped make railroads a practical and valuable form of transportation. Two of the most important were iron track and the "flanged" wheel, which has a rim around it to hold it onto the track. But the most important of all was the invention of the steam engine by James Watt in 1765. Before that, all cars were pulled by horses or mules.

The first railroads in the United States were built during the late 1820s.

They caused a lot of excitement. They were much faster than other forms of travel, and they could provide service year-round, unlike boats and stagecoaches. Trains were soon the main means of travel.

Railroads played a major part in the Industrial Revolution — the years of change when machines were first used to do work that had been done by hand for many centuries. Trains provided cheaper rates and quicker service for transporting goods. Because manufacturers could ship their goods over long distances, they could sell their products all over the nation instead of only in the surrounding cities and towns. This meant greater profits for the companies. Trains also brought people into the cities to work in factories.

Directions: Answer these questions about railroads.

1. What was used for power on the earliest railroads?_____

2. List three important developments that made railroads practical means of transportation.

1)_____ 2)_____ 3)_____

3. When were the first railroads built in America? _____

4. What is meant by "Industrial Revolution"? _____

_____

Locomotives

In the 1800s, the steam locomotive was considered by many to be a symbol of the new industrial age. It was, indeed, one of the most important inventions of the time. Over the years, there have been many changes on the locomotive. One of the most important has been its source of power. During its history, the locomotive has gone from steam to electric to diesel power.

The first railroads used horses for power. The development of the steam locomotive made railroads a practical means of transportation. The first steam locomotive was built in 1804 in Great Britain by Richard Trevithick. It could haul 50,000 pounds, but it was not very successful because it was too heavy. However, it encouraged other engineers to try to build steam locomotives. Two of the most important men to pick up the challenge were George Stephenson and his son, Robert. Robert once won a contest to build the best locomotive. "The Rocket", as he called it, had a top speed of 29 miles per hour.

In America, the developments were close behind those of the British. In 1830, Peter Cooper's tiny locomotive, called "Tom Thumb", lost a famous race against a horse-drawn coach. But it still convinced railroad officials that steam power was more practical than horse power.

Just before the turn of the century, the electric locomotive was widely used. At its peak in the 1940s, U.S. railroads had 2400 miles of electric routes.

The diesel locomotive was invented in the 1890s by Rudolf Diesel, a German engineer. The power of this locomotive was supplied by an oil-burning diesel engine. The diesel locomotive is still used today. It costs about twice as much as a steam locomotive to build, but it is much cheaper to operate.

Directions: Answer these questions about locomotives.

Check √

1. The main idea is:
   - ☐ The steam locomotive was considered a symbol of the industrial age.
   - ☐ Over the years, there have been many changes on the locomotive.

Write

2. Who built the first steam locomotive in 1804? _____

3. How fast could "The Rocket" travel? _____

4. Who built the locomotive called "Tom Thumb"? _____

5. "Tom Thumb" was in a race against a horse-drawn coach. Which won? _____

Railroad Pioneer

George Stephenson was born in Wylam, England, in 1781. His family was extremely poor. When he was young, he didn't go to school, but worked in the coal mines. In his spare time, he taught himself to read and write. After a series of explosions in the coal pits, Stephenson built a miners' safety lamp. This helped to bring him to the attention of the owners of the coal mines. They put him in charge of all the machinery.

In 1812, Stephenson became an engine builder for the mines. The owners were interested in locomotives because the cost of horse feed was so high. They told Stephenson to build a locomotive to pull the coal cars from the mines. His first locomotive, the Blucher, was put on the rails in 1814.

Stephenson was a good engineer, and he was fortunate to work for a rich employer. Between 1814 and 1826, Stephenson was the only man in all of Great Britain building locomotives.

When the Stockholm and Darlington Railway, the first public railroad system, was planned, Stephenson was named company engineer. He convinced the owners to use steam power instead of horses. He built the first locomotive on the line. The Locomotion, as it was called, was the best locomotive that had been built anywhere in the world up to that time. Over the years, Stephenson was responsible for many other important developments in locomotive design, such as improved cast-iron rails and wheels, and the first steel springs strong enough to carry several tons.

Stephenson was convinced that the future of railroads lay in steam power. His great vision of what the railroad system could become was a driving force in the early years of its development.

Directions: Answer these questions about railroads.

Circle **Yes** or **No**

1. George Stephenson was an excellent student in school.   Yes   No

2. Between 1814 and 1826, Stephenson was one of many engineers building locomotives in Great Britain.   Yes   No

3. The Stockholm and Darlington Railway was the first public railroad system.   Yes   No

4. The first locomotive on the Stockholm and Darlington line was the Locomotion, which was built by Stephenson.   Yes   No

Name: _____

A Steel-driving Man

A Tall Tale is a kind of legend. In these stories, each storyteller tries to "top" the others. The stories get more and more unbelievable. This one about John Henry is famous.

America had nearly 200,000 miles of track by 1900. Because of the rapid growth and the excitement over the railroads, many colorful stories about railroad heroes and adventures were told. Hammerman John Henry was such a hero. Here are some of the stories that were told about him.

On the night he was born, forked lightning split the air and the earth shook. He weighed forty-four pounds, and the first thing he did was to reach for a hammer hanging on the wall. "He's going to be a steel-driving man," his father told his mother.

One night John Henry dreamed he was working on a railroad. Every time his hammer hit a spike, the sky lit up with the sparks. "I dreamed that the railroad was going to be the end of me, and I'd die with a hammer in my hand," he said. John Henry did work for the railroads. He was the fastest, most powerful steel-driving man in the world.

In about 1870, the steam drill was invented. One day the company at the far end of a tunnel tried it out. John Henry's company, working at the other end, continued to use men to do the drilling. There was much bragging from both companies as to which was faster. Finally, they decided to have a contest. John Henry was matched against the best man with a steam drill.

John Henry was swinging a twenty-pound hammer in each hand. The sparks flew so fast and hot that they burned his face. At the end of the day, the judges said John Henry had beaten the steam drill by four feet! That night, John Henry said, "I was a steel-driving man." Then he laid down and closed his eyes forever.

Directions: Answer these questions about John Henry.

1. How much was John Henry said to have weighed at birth?_____

2. What invention was John Henry in a contest against? _____

3. What tools did John Henry use in the contest? _____

4. Who won the contest? _____

5. What happened to John Henry after the contest? _____

Name: _____

Passenger Cars

The early railroad passenger cars were little more than stagecoaches fitted with special wheels to help them stay on the tracks. They didn't hold many passengers, and because they were made out of wood, they were fire **hazards**. They also did not hold up very well if the train came off the track or had a **collision** with another train.

In the United States, it wasn't long before passenger cars were lengthened to hold more people. Late in the 1830s, Americans were riding in **elongated** cars with double seats on either side of a center aisle. By the early 1900s, most cars were made of metal instead of wood.

Sleeping and dining cars were introduced in the United States by the early 1860s. Over the next twenty-five years, other improvements were made including electric lighting, steam heat, and covered **vestibules** that allowed passengers to walk between cars. All of these **luxeries** helped to make railroad travel much more comfortable.

Directions: Answer these questions about passenger cars.

Check √

1. Based on the other words in the sentence, what is the correct definition for "hazards"?
   - ☐ engines
   - ☐ risks
   - ☐ stations

2. Based on the other words in the sentence, what is the correct definition for "collision"?
   - ☐ crash
   - ☐ race
   - ☐ track

3. Based on the other words in the sentence, what is the correct definition for "elongated"?
   - ☐ wooden
   - ☐ new
   - ☐ lengthened

4. Based on the other words in the sentence, what is the correct definition for "vestibules"?
   - ☐ passageways
   - ☐ cars
   - ☐ depots

5. Based on the other words in the sentence, what is the correct definition for "luxuries"?
   - ☐ additions
   - ☐ things offering the greatest comfort
   - ☐ inventions

Name: _____

Review

When railroads became the major means of transportation, they replaced earlier forms of travel, such as the stagecoach. Railroads were the unchallenged leader for a hundred years. But beginning in the early 1900s, railroads have faced **competition** from newer forms of transportation.

Today millions of people have their own automobiles. Buses offer inexpensive travel between cities. Large trucks are used for hauling goods. Airplanes provide quick transportation over long distances. The result has been a sharp drop in the use of trains.

Nearly all railroads face serious problems that threaten to drive them out of business. But railroads provide low-cost, fuel-saving transportation that will remain important. One gallon of diesel fuel will haul about four times as much by railroad as by truck. In a time when the world is concerned about saving fuel, this is but one area in which the railroads still have much to offer.

Directions: Answer these questions about railroads.

Check √

1. The main idea is:
   ☐ When railroads became the major means of transportation, they replaced earlier forms of travel.
   ☐ Beginning in the early 1900s, railroads have faced competition from newer forms of transportation.

2. Based on the other words in the sentence, what is the correct definition for "competition"?
   ☐ businesses trying to get the same customers
   ☐ problems
   ☐ support

Write

3. Name four newer forms of transportation that have challenged railroads.

1)_____   2)_____

3)_____   4)_____

Circle Yes or No

4. One gallon of diesel fuel will haul about twice as much by railroad as by truck.   Yes   No

Raining Cats and Dogs

An idiom is an expression that means something different than the words in it.
The story below is full of idioms.
Read the entire story first.
Then reread it and underline all the idioms you find.

It was raining cats and dogs as Kim and Tomi approached the old wooden house. "This is getting on my nerves," Tomi said.

"Don't be such a scaredy cat," teased Kim. "We're just going to collect paper route money from grumpy Mr. Hendon."

"I know, but just don't shoot off your mouth like last time," mumbled Tomi.

"Well, he really got my goat the way he teased about that hornet's nest on the porch," Kim responded. "Anyway, we're here now. Might as well face the music."

Kim and Tomi went up the steps and rang the doorbell. Nothing happened. "Are we on a wild goose chase?" asked Kim. She rang the bell two more times.

"Hold your horses," shouted a voice from inside. Then there was some loud stomping and rattling.

"Let's call it a day," said Tomi nervously.

"You're not going to chicken out now," said Kim, grabbing her brother's hand.

Finally, the door swung open. A tall wire-haired man stared down at them with darts in his eyes. "Here to rip me off? What are you up to?" he demanded.

"Uh, just collecting money for the Daily Blattle," said Tomi, his knees knocking together.

Mr. Hendon's face suddenly became sunny. "Ah! I thought you were some of those kids who have been giving me a hard time. They were horsing around on the porch roof, and one almost broke a leg when she fell. Scared the pants off me. Well, now, wait right here. I'll get your money in just two winks."

How many idioms did you find? _____
How did you do?   0–5 Try again.   11–15 Good reading!
                 6–10 Not bad.   16 or more Super!

Now draw a picture for one of the idioms.
Show what the words usually mean, *not* what the idiom means.

Identifying idioms

Crosswords

Read each clue.
Decide what word completes the sentence and fits in the
crossword puzzle.
Write the answer in the puzzle.

Across

2. *Hand* is to _____ as *foot* is to *toe*.

3. *Hot* is to _____ as *cold* is to *ice*.

4. *Easy* is to *simple* as _____ is to *difficult*.

6. *Cow* is to *milk* as *bee* is to _____.

7. *Bicycle* is to _____ as *car* is to *four*.

9. _____ is to *big* as *lowercase* is to *small*.

13. *Carve* is to *knife* as *write* is to _____.

14. *Woman* is to _____ as *man* is to *men*.

Down

1. *Fruit* is to *peach* as _____ is to *carrot*.

2. *Penny* is to *one* as *nickel* is to _____.

3. *Shell* is to _____ as *fur* is to *cat*.

5. *Pizza* is to *food* as _____ is to *toy*.

6. _____ is to *sad* as *up* is to *down*.

8. *Mississippi* is to *river* as *Atlantic* is to _____.

10. *Lead* is to *pencil* as _____ is to *pen*.

11. _____ is to *plane* as *water* is to *boat*.

12. *Year* is to *day* as *hour* is to _____.

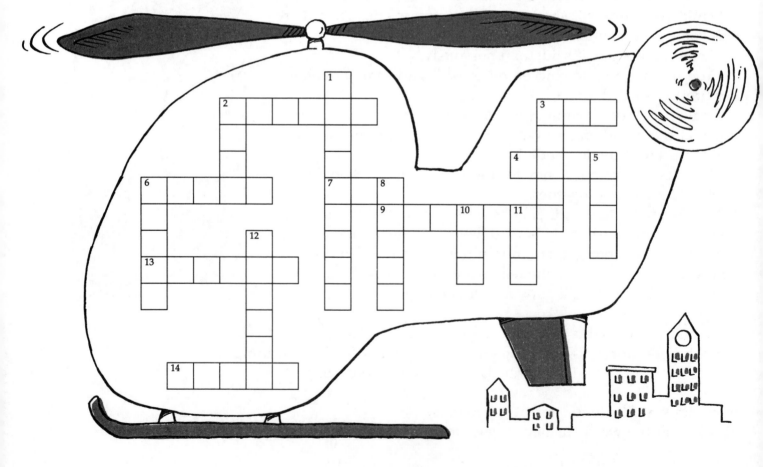

Completing analogies

Figure It Out

What can you figure out from each short passage below?
Circle the letter of the conclusion you think is best.
When you are finished, compare your answers with your classmates.
Discuss why you chose each answer.

1. Phillip sank back into his seat, relieved. Dust from the exploded meteor swirled past the windows. "That was a close call!" he thought.

   a. Phillip is a taxi cab driver.
   b. Phillip is a window washer.
   c. Phillip is a space pilot.

2. The lump under the covers started to move. When it reached the end of the bed, a streak of fur raced out and darted across the room.

   a. A lumpy bed had come to life and moved around the room.
   b. Someone had made up the bed with a cat inside.
   c. A cat had run into the room and was hiding under the bed.

3. Stella pedaled steadily for the first several laps. She coasted when going downhill. Then, as she approached the finish line, she gathered all her energy and pumped as hard as she could.

   a. Stella is swimming in a pool.
   b. Stella is lifting weights.
   c. Stella is riding in a bicycle race.

4. "I want to see how quickly you respond," Pedro said to Dana. He held the ruler so that the bottom was just between Dana's fingers. Then he let go and Dana caught the ruler. "Three inches," Pedro said.

   a. Pedro was doing an experiment.
   b. Pedro was measuring Dana's fingers.
   c. Pedro was making rulers.

5. Uri's eyelids began to flutter and droop. He could still hear the construction equipment making a racket next door. "Not a wink all night. When are they going to stop?" he asked.

   a. Uri had stayed up all night working next door.
   b. Uri had been kept up all night by noisy construction.
   c. Uri was on a construction crew that worked at night.

Inferring conclusions

Fable Maze

In each pair of sentences below, one sentence tells a cause and the other sentence tells the effect.

Mark each sentence **C** for *cause* or **E** for *effect*.

1. ____ The fox leaped into the air with its jaws open.
   ____ A bunch of juicy grapes hung high up, just out of reach.

2. ____ The lion was trapped in the net, unable to move.
   ____ The hunters dropped their net on the mighty lion.

3. ____ The moon was always changing from thin to full and round.
   ____ The moon's mother could not make a gown to fit her.

4. ____ During the race, the hare went to sleep under a tree.
   ____ The hare lost the race to the tortoise.

5. ____ The fox made the crow want to prove it had a lovely voice.
   ____ The crow opened its mouth to sing and dropped the cheese.

6. ____ When the weather turned cold, the man was freezing.
   ____ The man sold his coat to the first person he met on the road.

Now complete the maze.
Begin at START and look at the first pair of sentences.
If the first sentence is the cause, follow the green arrow.
If the first sentence is the effect, follow the black arrow.
Each time you come to a star, use the next pair of sentences to find out which way to go.

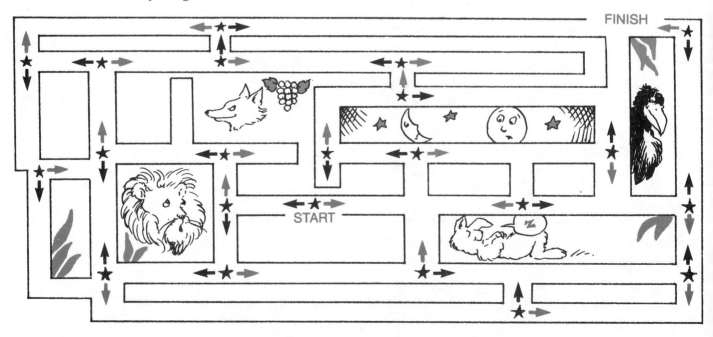

Identifying causes and effects

Character Words

Read each paragraph below.
Notice what the character says, thinks, feels, and does.
Then look at the words in the middle of the page.
Draw a line from the paragraph to each word that describes
the character.
You may use some words more than once.

Rachel bounded into the room and began shouting. "Guess what everbody! I made the volleyball team! Coach said I'm a natural. She said I have great promise." By now, Rachel had shrugged off her coat, which landed on the floor. She had tossed her books onto the kitchen table, and they had scattered in every direction. "I hope I can do it," thought Rachel. "Everybody thinks I'm such a great player. I hope I don't let them down."

Mel had never been so scared in his life. He stared at the rattlesnake just a foot or so from his left boot. "Freeze, don't move," he kept thinking to himself. "You know what to do. Do nothing. Stay calm. It's only another frightened creature like me," he told himself. The rattler, unable to see Mel unless he moved, finally slithered away. Back at camp, someone asked Mel what he had been doing. "Oh, nothing," Mel said with a smile.

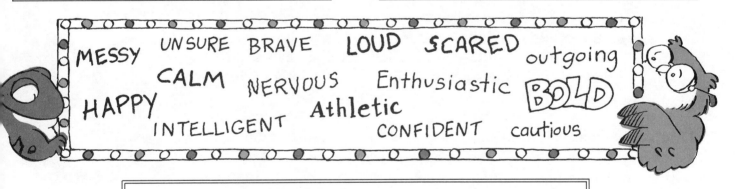

MESSY   UNSURE   BRAVE   LOUD   SCARED   outgoing
CALM   NERVOUS   Enthusiastic   BOLD
HAPPY   Athletic
INTELLIGENT   CONFIDENT   cautious

Lydia really wasn't too sure she was doing the right thing, but anything was worth a try. "Besides," she thought to herself, "I've got a feeling this is going to work out." She held the package tightly, as if it might get away. Finally, the secretary showed her in. At last! She was entering the office of the president of the largest toy company in the world! She looked the president in the eye and said confidently, "I've invented a toy you will just love. It will turn out to be the toy of the century, I'm sure!"

Analyzing characters

Who's Telling?

Read each paragraph below.
Decide who is telling the story.

A A character who is in the story.
B A narrator who is not a character in the story.
C A narrator who is also a character, referred to by the word *I*.

Write **A**, **B**, or **C** in front of each paragraph to show who is telling the story.

1. ____ Nancy and Lonnie had not spoken to each other in months. Things had started out innocently enough. Lonnie had teased Nancy about her red hair. She seemed to go along with it for a few days. But then Lonnie found his locker filled with shaving cream. That's when they had this big fight.

2. ____ What could that be crawling along the floor? Kane squinted. Nuts! He had forgotten his glasses this morning. Kane squinted harder, as if by muscle power he could see better. He was startled by a tap on his shoulder. "Kane," said the science teacher. "Where is the mouse you were studying?"

3. ____ The space freighter was hardly gleaming and new. The carpet on the inside was soiled and torn in places. Someone had spilled juice on the computer, and the keys on the keyboard stuck at times. The whole ship smelled funny. "Another pile of junk to pilot," I thought as I signed the work order.

4. ____ The quarrel had to stop. At recess I wandered out into the schoolyard. There was Nancy, talking to some friends. And there was Lonnie, sitting on a bench eating an apple. It was now or never. I caught Lonnie's eye and motioned for him to come over.

5. ____ Free at last! The little creature scooted along the floor over by the wall, hoping the Big Thing that had yanked its tail would not notice. It seemed to be trying to make it to the door. It stopped for a moment, wiggling its whiskers and testing the air for danger.

Which paragraphs could be from the same story?
Write the numbers of the paragraphs that go together.   ____ and ____   ____ and ____

Identifying a story's point of view

ANSWER KEY

MASTER READING
5

Adding Suffixes

The suffixes **-ant** and **-ent** mean a person or thing that does something. Example, one who occupies a place is the occup**ant**.

Directions: Combine each root word and suffix to make a new word. (When a word ends in silent **e**, keep the **e** before adding a suffix beginning with a consonant. Drop the **e** before adding a suffix beginning with a vowel.)

Example: announce + ment = announcement; announce + ing + announcing.) The first one is done for you.

ROOT WORD	SUFFIX	NEW WORD
observe	-ant	observant
contest	-ant	contestant
please	-ant	pleasant
preside	-ent	president
differ	-ent	different

Directions: Using the meanings in the parentheses, complete each sentence with one of the words you just formed. One is done for you.

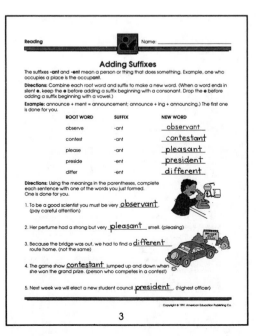

1. To be a good scientist you must be very **observant**. (pay careful attention)

2. Her perfume had a strong but very **pleasant** smell. (pleasing)

3. Because the bridge was out, we had to find a **different** route home. (not the same)

4. The game show **contestant** jumped up and down when she won the grand prize. (person who competes in a contest)

5. Next week we will elect a new student council **president**. (highest officer)

3

Make New Words

The suffix **-al** means of, like, or suitable for; **-ative** means having the nature of or relating to; **-ive** means have or tend to be.

Directions: Combine each root word and suffix to form a new word. Remember that the spelling of the root word sometimes changes when a suffix is added. The first one is done for you.

ROOT WORD	SUFFIX	NEW WORD
logic	-al	logical
imagine	-ative	imaginative
talk	-ative	talkative
impress	-ive	impressive
attract	-ive	attractive

Directions: Using the meanings in the parentheses, complete each sentence with one of the words you just formed.

1. Because of his acting ability, Michael was the **logical** choice to have the lead part in the school play. (decided with reasoning)

2. Our history teacher is a rather **talkative** man, who likes to tell jokes and stories. (fond of talking)

3. That book has such an **imaginative** plot! (showing imagination)

4. Monica thought the dress in the store window was very **attractive**. (pleasing, something that attracts)

5. The high school basketball team was **impressive** in its Friday night game, beating their rivals by thirty points. (making an impression on the mind or emotions)

4

Changing The Meanings Of Words

The prefixes **il-**, **im-**, **in-**, and **ir-** all mean not.

Directions: Divide each word into its prefix and root word. The first one is done for you.

	PREFIX	ROOT WORD
illogical	il	logical
impatient	im	patient
immature	im	mature
incomplete	in	complete
insincere	in	sincere
irresponsible	ir	responsible
irregular	ir	regular

Directions: Using the meanings in the parentheses, complete each sentence with one of the words you just formed.

1. I had to turn in my assignment **incomplete** because I was sick last night. (not finished)

2. It was **illogical** for Jimmy to give me his keys because he can't get into his house without them. (not reasonable)

3. Sue and Joel were **irresponsible** to have a party while there parents were out of town. (lacking a sense of responsibility)

4. I sometimes get **impatient** waiting for my ride to school. (a lack of patience)

5. The boys sounded **insincere** when they said they were sorry. (not honest)

6. These pants didn't cost much because they are **irregular**. (not straight or even)

5

Similes

Directions: Choose a word from the word box to complete each comparison. One is done for you.

tack	grass	fish	mule	ox	rail	hornet	monkey

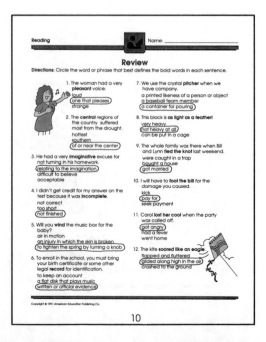

1. as stubborn as a **mule**
2. as strong as an **ox**
3. swims like a **fish**
4. as sharp as a **tack**
5. as thin as a **rail**
6. as mad as a **hornet**
7. climbs like a **monkey**
8. as green as **grass**

Directions: Use words of your own to complete the following similes.

1. as **sharp (answers vary)** as a tack
2. as light as a _____
3. _____ like a bird
4. as _____ as honey
5. as hungry as a _____
6. as _____ like a snake
7. as white as _____
8. as cold as _____

Directions: Make up similes to finish the following sentences.

1. Our new puppy sounded **Answers Vary**
2. The clouds were _____
3. Our new car is _____
4. The watermelon tasted _____

8

Homographs

Directions: Write the definition from the box for the bold word in each sentence.

pres ent	n.	a gift
pre sent	v.	to introduce or offer to view
rec ord	n.	written or official evidence
re cord	v.	to keep an account of
wind	n.	air in motion
wind	v.	to tighten the spring by turning a knob, as with a watch
wound (woond)	n.	an injury in which the skin is broken
wound	v.	past tense of wind

1. I would like to **present** our new student council president, Mindy Hall.
   To introduce or offer to view.

2. The store made a **record** of all my payments.
   Written or official evidence.

3. Don't forget to **wind** your alarm clock before you go to sleep.
   To tighten the spring by turning a knob.

4. He received a serious **wound** on his hand by playing with a knife.
   An injury in which the skin is broken.

5. The **wind** knocked over my bicycle.
   Air in motion.

6. I bought her a birthday **present** with my allowance.
   A gift.

6

Figurative Language

Directions: Write the letter of the correct meaning for the bold words in each sentence. One is done for you.

a. refusal to see or listen	f. pay for
b. misbehaving, acting in a wild way	g. unknowing
c. made a thoughtless remark	h. feeling very sad
d. lost an opportunity	i. get married
e. got angry	j. excited and happy

f 1. My parents will **foot the bill** for my birthday party.

i 2. Tony and Lisa will finally **tie the knot** in June.

h 3. Sam was **down in the dumps** after he wrecked his bicycle.

c 4. Sarah **put her foot in her mouth** when she was talking to our teacher.

d 5. I really **missed the boat** when I turned down the chance to work after school.

a 6. I got the **brush off** from Susan when I tried to ask her where she was last night.

g 7. Mickey is **in the dark** about our plans to throw a surprise birthday party for him.

b 8. The children were **bouncing off the walls** when the babysitter was trying to put them to bed.

j 9. The students were **flying high** on the last day of school.

e 10. My sister **lost her cool** when she found out that I spilled chocolate milk on her new sweater.

9

What Is The Correct Meaning?

Directions: Circle the correct definition of the bold word in each sentence. One is done for you.

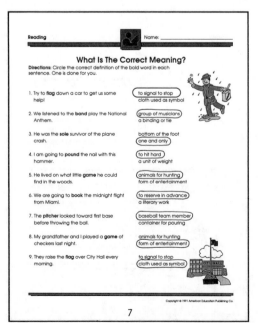

1. Try to **flag** down a car to get us some help!
   - (to signal to stop)
   - cloth used as symbol

2. We listened to the **band** play the National Anthem.
   - (group of musicians)
   - a binding or tie

3. He was the **sole** survivor of the plane crash.
   - bottom of the foot
   - (one and only)

4. I am going to **pound** the nail with this hammer.
   - (to hit hard)
   - a unit of weight

5. He lived on what little **game** he could find in the woods.
   - (animals for hunting)
   - form of entertainment

6. We are going to **book** the midnight flight from Miami.
   - (to reserve in advance)
   - a literary work

7. The **pitcher** looked toward first base before throwing the ball.
   - (baseball team member)
   - container for pouring

8. My grandfather and I played a **game** of checkers last night.
   - animals for hunting
   - (form of entertainment)

9. They raise the **flag** over City Hall every morning.
   - to signal to stop
   - (cloth used as symbol)

7

Review

Directions: Circle the word or phrase that best defines the bold words in each sentence.

1. The woman had a very **pleasant** voice.
   - loud
   - (one that pleases)
   - strange

2. The **central** regions of the country suffered most from the drought.
   - hottest
   - southern
   - (of or near the center)

3. He had a very **imaginative** excuse for not turning in his homework.
   - (relating to the imagination)
   - difficult to believe
   - acceptable

4. I didn't get credit for my answer on the test because it was **incomplete**.
   - not correct
   - too short
   - (not finished)

5. Will you **wind** the music box for the baby?
   - air in motion
   - an injury in which the skin is broken
   - (to tighten the spring by turning a knob)

6. To enroll in the school, you must bring your birth certificate or some other legal **record** for identification.
   - to keep an account
   - a flat disk that plays music
   - (written or official evidence)

7. We use the crystal **pitcher** when we have company.
   - a printed likeness of a person or object
   - a baseball team member
   - (a container for pouring)

8. This block is **as light as a feather!**
   - very heavy
   - (not heavy at all)
   - can be put in a cage

9. The whole family was there when Bill and Lynn **tied the knot** last weekend.
   - were caught in a trap
   - bought a house
   - (got married)

10. I will have to **foot the bill** for the damage you caused.
    - kick
    - (pay for)
    - seek payment

11. Carol **lost her cool** when the party was called off.
    - (got angry)
    - had a fever
    - went home

12. The kite **soared like an eagle**.
    - flapped and fluttered
    - (glided along high in the air)
    - crashed to the ground

10

Page 11

Find The Words

Directions: Find each of the words from the word box in the puzzle. Some words go across, some go up and down, one is on the diagonal, and two are backwards. One is done for you.

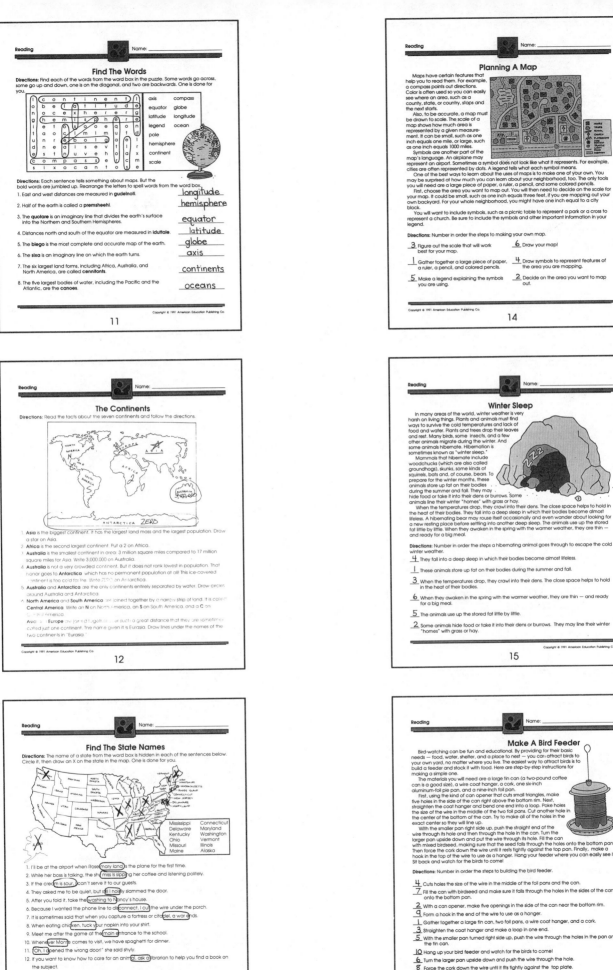

axis	compass
equator	globe
latitude	longitude
legend	ocean
pole	
hemisphere	
continent	
scale	

Directions: Each sentence tells something about maps. But the bold words are jumbled up. Rearrange the letters to spell words from the word box.

1. East and west distances are measured in **gudelnoti**.   _longitude_

2. Half of the earth is called a **premsheehi**.   _hemisphere_

3. The **quotare** is an imaginary line that divides the earth's surface into the Northern and Southern Hemispheres.   _equator_

4. Distances north and south of the equator are measured in **iduttale**.   _latitude_

5. The **blego** is the most complete and accurate map of the earth.   _globe_

6. The **sixa** is an imaginary line on which the earth turns.   _axis_

7. The six largest land forms, including Africa, Australia, and North America, are called **cennitonts**.   _continents_

8. The five largest bodies of water, including the Pacific and the Atlantic, are the **canoes**.   _oceans_

11

Page 12

The Continents

Directions: Read the facts about the seven continents and follow the directions.

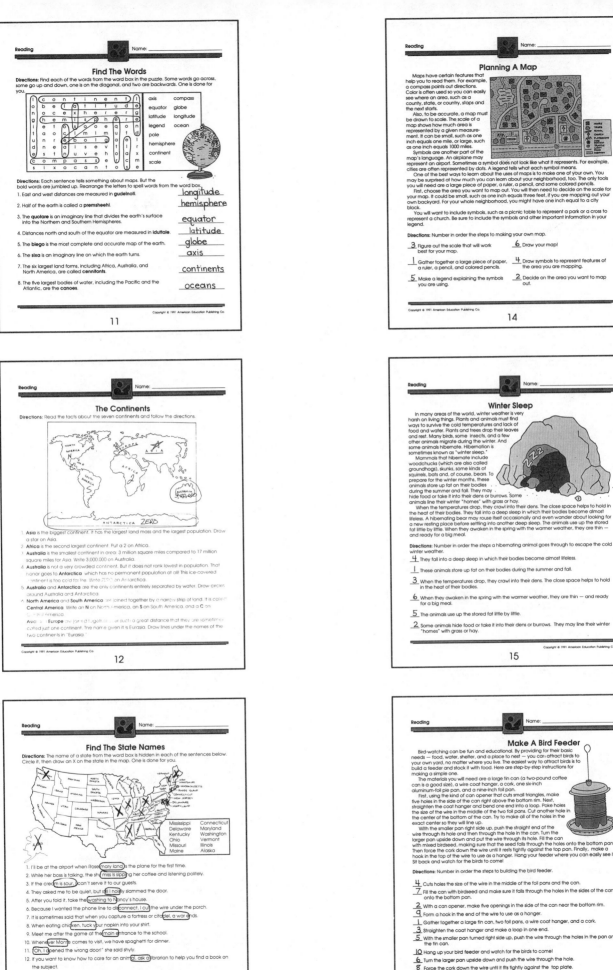

1. **Asia** is the biggest continent. It has the largest land mass and the largest population. Draw a star on Asia.

2. **Africa** is the second largest continent. Put a 2 on Africa.

3. **Australia** is the smallest continent in area: 3 million square miles compared to 17 million square miles for Asia. Write 3,000,000 on Australia.

4. **Australia** is not a very crowded continent. But it does not rank lowest in population. That honor goes to **Antarctica** which has no permanent population at all! This ice-covered continent is too cold for life. Write ZERO on Antarctica.

5. **Australia** and **Antarctica** are the only continents entirely separated by water. Draw circles around Australia and Antarctica.

6. **North America** and **South America** are joined together by a narrow strip of land. It is called **Central America**. Write an N on North America, an S on South America, and a C on Central America.

7. **Asia** and **Europe** are joined together in such a great distance that they are sometimes called just one continent. The name given is Eurasia. Draw lines under the names of the two continents in "Eurasia."

12

Page 13

Find The State Names

Directions: The name of a state from the word box is hidden in each of the sentences below. Circle it, then draw an X on the state in the map. One is done for you.

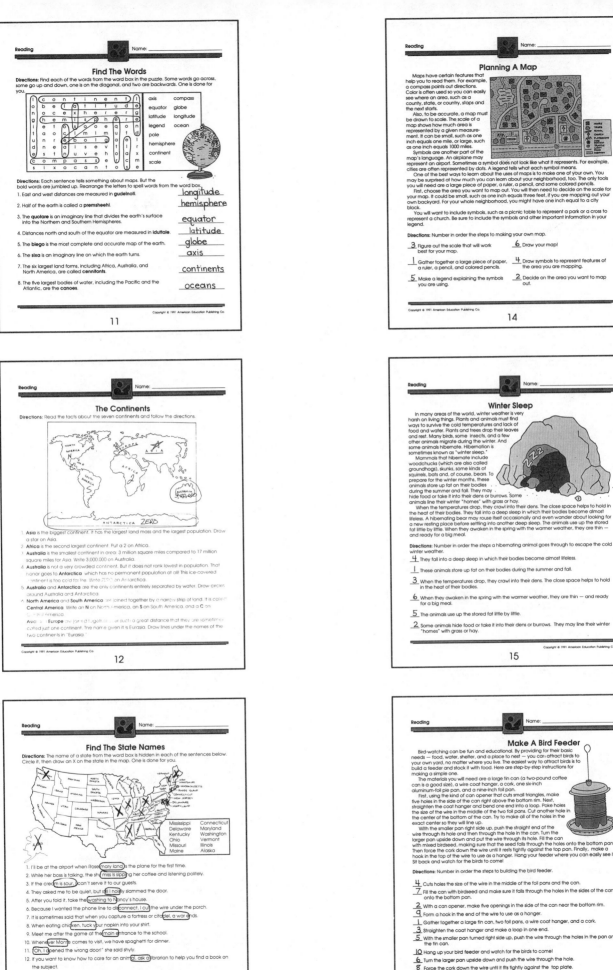

Mississippi	Connecticut
Delaware	Maryland
Kentucky	Washington
Ohio	Vermont
Missouri	Illinois
Maine	Alaska

1. I'll be at the airport when Rosemary lands the plane for the first time.
2. While her boss is talking, the shy miss is sipping her coffee and listening politely.
3. If the cream is sour, I can't serve it to our guests.
4. They asked me to be quiet, but still I noisily slammed the door.
5. After you fold it, take the washing to Nancy's house.
6. Because I wanted the phone line to disconnect, I cut the wire under the porch.
7. It is sometimes said that when you capture a fortress or citadel, a war ends.
8. When eating chicken, tuck your napkin into your shirt.
9. Meet me after the game at the main entrance to the school.
10. Whenever Monte comes to visit, we have spaghetti for dinner.
11. "Oh, I opened the wrong door!" she said shyly.
12. If you want to know how to care for an animal, ask a librarian to help you find a book on the subject.

13

Page 14

Planning A Map

Maps have certain features that help you to read them. For example, a compass points out directions. Color is often used so you can easily see where an area, such as a county, state, or country, stops and the next starts.

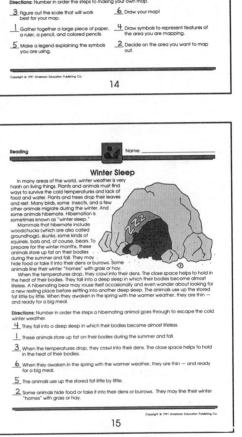

Also, to be accurate, a map must be drawn to scale. The scale of a map shows how much area is represented by a given measurement. It can be small, such as one inch equals one mile, or large, such as one inch equals 1000 miles.

Symbols are another part of the map's language. An airplane may represent an airport. Sometimes a symbol does not look like what it represents. For example, cities are often represented by dots. A legend tells what each symbol means.

One of the best ways to learn about the uses of maps is to make one of your own. You may be surprised at how much you can learn about your neighborhood, too. The only tools you will need are a large piece of paper, a ruler, a pencil, and some colored pencils.

First, choose the area you want to map out. You will then need to decide on the scale for your map. It could be small, such as one inch equals three feet, if you are mapping out your own backyard. For your whole neighborhood, you might have one inch equal to a city block.

You will want to include symbols, such as a picnic table to represent a park or a cross to represent a church. Be sure to include the symbols and other important information in your legend.

Directions: Number in order the steps to making your own map.

3   Figure out the scale that will work best for your map.

1   Gather together a large piece of paper, a ruler, a pencil, and colored pencils.

5   Make a legend explaining the symbols you are using.

6   Draw your map!

4   Draw symbols to represent features of the area you are mapping.

2   Decide on the area you want to map out.

14

Page 15

Winter Sleep

In many areas of the world, winter weather is very harsh on living things. Plants and animals must find ways to survive the cold temperatures and lack of food and water. Plants and trees drop their leaves and rest. Many birds, some insects, and a few other animals migrate during the winter. And some animals hibernate. Hibernation is sometimes known as "winter sleep."

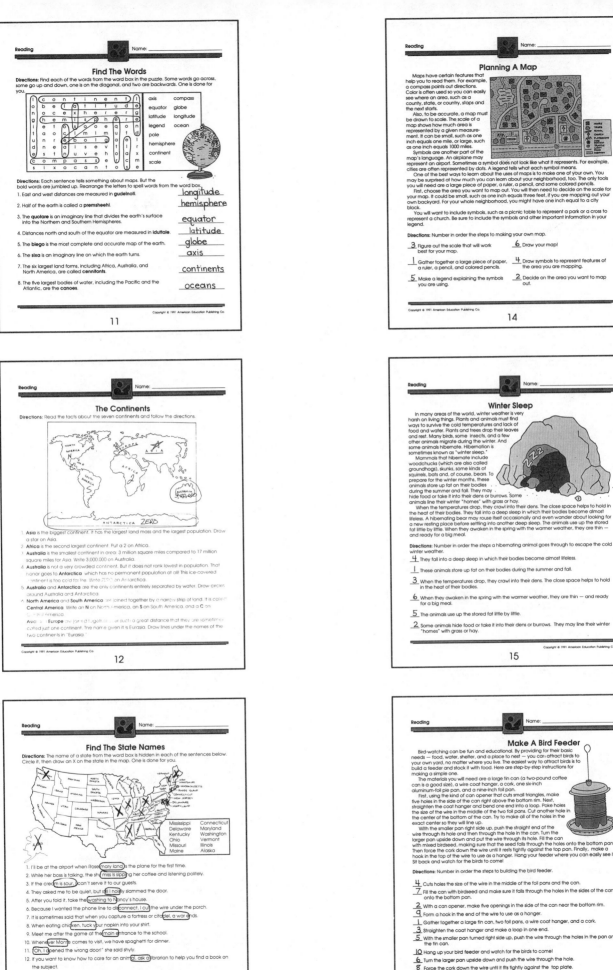

Mammals that hibernate include woodchucks (which are also called groundhogs), skunks, some kinds of squirrels, bats and, of course, bears. To prepare for the winter months, these animals store up fat on their bodies during the summer and fall. They may hide food or take it into their dens or burrows. Some animals line their winter "homes" with grass or hay.

When the temperatures drop, they crawl into their dens or burrows. The close space helps to hold in the heat of their bodies. They fall into a deep sleep in which their bodies become almost lifeless. A hibernating bear may rouse itself occasionally and even wander about looking for a new resting place before settling into another deep sleep. The animals use up the stored fat little by little. When they awaken in the spring with the warmer weather, they are thin — and ready for a big meal.

Directions: Number in order the steps a hibernating animal goes through to escape the cold winter weather.

4   They fall into a deep sleep in which their bodies become almost lifeless.

1   These animals store up fat on their bodies during the summer and fall.

3   When the temperatures drop, they crawl into their dens. The close space helps to hold in the heat of their bodies.

6   When they awaken in the spring with the warmer weather, they are thin — and ready for a big meal.

5   The animals use up the stored fat little by little.

2   Some animals hide food or take it into their dens or burrows. They may line their winter "homes" with grass or hay.

15

Page 16

Make A Bird Feeder

Bird-watching can be fun and educational. By providing for their basic needs — food, water, shelter, and a place to nest — you can attract birds to your own yard, no matter where you live. The easiest way to attract birds is to build a feeder and stock it with food. Here are step-by-step instructions for making a simple one.

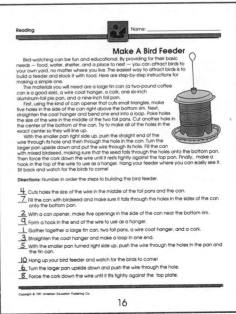

The materials you will need are a large tin can (a two-pound coffee can is a good size), a wire coat hanger, a cork, one six-inch aluminum-foil pie pan, and a nine-inch foil pan.

First, using the kind of can opener that cuts small triangles, make five holes in the side of the can right above the bottom rim. Next, straighten the coat hanger and bend one end into a loop. Poke holes the size of the wire in the middle of the two foil pans. Cut another hole in the center of the bottom of the can. Try to make all of the holes in the exact center so they will line up.

With the smaller pan right side up, push the straight end of the wire through its hole and then through the hole in the can. Turn the larger pan upside down and put the wire through its hole. Fill the can with mixed birdseed, making sure that the seed falls through the holes onto the bottom pan. Then force the cork down the wire until it rests tightly against the top pan. Finally, make a hook in the top of the wire to use as a hanger. Hang your feeder where you can easily see it. Sit back and watch for the birds to come!

Directions: Number in order the steps to building the bird feeder.

4   Cuts holes the size of the wire in the middle of the foil pans and the can.

7   Fill the can with birdseed and make sure it falls through the holes in the sides of the can onto the bottom pan.

2   With a can opener, make five openings in the side of the can near the bottom rim.

9   Form a hook in the end of the wire to use as a hanger.

1   Gather together a large tin can, two foil pans, a wire coat hanger, and a cork.

3   Straighten the coat hanger and make a loop in one end.

5   With the smaller pan turned right side up, push the wire through the holes in the pan and the tin can.

10   Hang up your bird feeder and watch for the birds to come!

6   Turn the larger pan upside down and push the wire through the hole.

8   Force the cork down the wire until it fits tightly against the top plate.

16

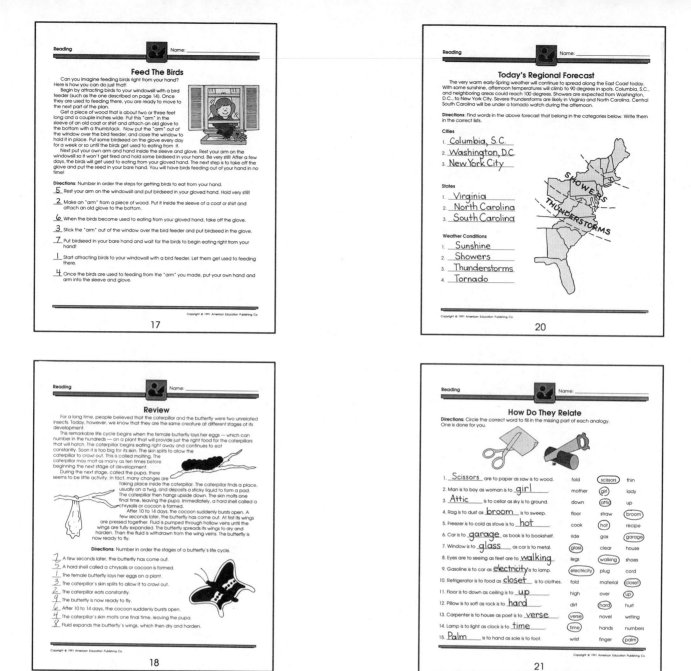

Feed The Birds

Can you imagine feeding birds right from your hand? Here is how you can do just that!

Begin by attracting birds to your windowsill with a bird feeder (such as the one described on page 14). Once they are used to feeding there, you are ready to move to the next part of the plan.

Get a piece of wood that is about two or three feet long and a couple inches wide. Put this "arm" in the sleeve of an old coat or shirt and attach an old glove to the bottom with a thumbtack. Now put the "arm" out of the window over the bird feeder, and close the window to hold it in place. Put some birdseed on the glove every day for a week or so until the birds get used to eating from it.

Next put your own arm and hand inside the sleeve and glove. Rest your arm on the windowsill so it won't get tired and hold some birdseed in your hand. Be very still! After a few days, the birds will get used to eating from your gloved hand. The next step is to take off the glove and put the seed in your bare hand. You will have birds eating out of your hand in no time!

Directions: Number in order the steps for getting birds to eat from your hand.

5 Rest your arm on the windowsill and put birdseed in your gloved hand. Hold very still!

2 Make an "arm" from a piece of wood. Put it inside the sleeve of a coat or shirt and attach an old glove to the bottom.

6 When the birds become used to eating from your gloved hand, take off the glove.

3 Stick the "arm" out of the window over the bird feeder and put birdseed in the glove.

7 Put birdseed in your bare hand and wait for the birds to begin eating right from your hand!

1 Start attracting birds to your windowsill with a bird feeder. Let them get used to feeding there.

4 Once the birds are used to feeding from the "arm" you made, put your own hand and arm into the sleeve and glove.

17

Today's Regional Forecast

The very warm early-Spring weather will continue to spread along the East Coast today. With some sunshine, afternoon temperatures will climb to 90 degrees in spots. Columbia, S.C., and neighboring areas could reach 100 degrees. Showers are expected from Washington, D.C., to New York City. Severe thunderstorms are likely in Virginia and North Carolina. Central South Carolina will be under a tornado watch during the afternoon.

Directions: Find words in the above forecast that belong in the categories below. Write them in the correct lists.

Cities
1. Columbia, S.C.
2. Washington, D.C.
3. New York City

States
1. Virginia
2. North Carolina
3. South Carolina

Weather Conditions
1. Sunshine
2. Showers
3. Thunderstorms
4. Tornado

20

Review

For a long time, people believed that the caterpillar and the butterfly were two unrelated insects. Today, however, we know that they are the same creature at different stages of its development.

This remarkable life cycle begins when the female butterfly lays her eggs — which can number in the hundreds — on a plant that will provide just the right food for the caterpillars that will hatch. The caterpillar begins eating right away and continues to eat constantly. Soon it is too big for its skin. The skin splits to allow the caterpillar to crawl out. This is called molting. The caterpillar may molt as many as ten times before beginning the next stage of development.

During the next stage, called the pupa, there seems to be little activity. In fact, many changes are taking place inside the caterpillar. The caterpillar finds a place, usually on a twig, and deposits a sticky liquid to form a pad. The caterpillar then hangs upside down. The skin molts one final time, leaving the pupa. Immediately, a hard shell called a chrysalis or cocoon is formed.

After 10 to 14 days, the cocoon suddenly bursts open. A few seconds later, the butterfly has come out. At first its wings are pressed together. Fluid is pumped through hollow veins until the wings are fully expanded. The butterfly spreads its wings to dry and harden. Then the fluid is withdrawn from the wing veins. The butterfly is now ready to fly.

Directions: Number in order the stages of a butterfly's life cycle.

7 A few seconds later, the butterfly has come out.

5 A hard shell called a chrysalis or cocoon is formed.

1 The female butterfly lays her eggs on a plant.

3 The caterpillar's skin splits to allow it to crawl out.

2 The caterpillar eats constantly.

9 The butterfly is now ready to fly.

6 After 10 to 14 days, the cocoon suddenly bursts open.

4 The caterpillar's skin molts one final time, leaving the pupa.

8 Fluid expands the butterfly's wings, which then dry and harden.

18

How Do They Relate

Directions: Circle the correct word to fill in the missing part of each analogy. One is done for you.

1. Scissors are to paper as saw is to wood.   fold   (scissors)   thin
2. Man is to boy as woman is to girl.   mother   (girl)   lady
3. Attic is to cellar as sky is to ground.   down   (attic)   up
4. Rag is to dust as broom is to sweep.   floor   straw   (broom)
5. Freezer is to cold as stove is to hot.   cook   (hot)   recipe
6. Car is to garage as book is to bookshelf.   ride   gas   (garage)
7. Window is to glass as car is to metal.   (glass)   clear   house
8. Eyes are to seeing as feet are to walking.   legs   (walking)   shoes
9. Gasoline is to car as electricity is to lamp.   (electricity)   plug   cord
10. Refrigerator is to food as closet is to clothes.   fold   material   (closet)
11. Floor is to down as ceiling is to up.   high   over   (up)
12. Pillow is to soft as rock is to hard.   dirt   (hard)   hurt
13. Carpenter is to house as poet is to verse.   (verse)   novel   writing
14. Lamp is to light as clock is to time.   (time)   hands   numbers
15. Palm is to hand as sole is to foot.   wrist   finger   (palm)

21

What Are They?

Directions: Read each group of words. Cross out the word that does not belong. Then add a word of your own that does belong. One is done for you.

1. wren   robin   ~~feather~~   sparrow   eagle   **bluebird**
2. sofa   stool   chair   ~~carpet~~   bench   **answers will vary**
3. lettuce   ~~salad~~   corn   broccoli   spinach
4. pencil   chalk   crayon   pen   ~~drawing~~
5. perch   shark   ~~penguin~~   bass   tuna
6. rapid   quick   ~~unhurried~~   swift   speedy
7. lemon   ~~daisy~~   melon   lime   grapefruit

Directions: Above each group of words, write a category name from the word box. Then write a word of your own that belongs in each group.

storms
blizzard
hurricane
thunder
lightening (these will vary)

parts of the leg
ankle
shin
thigh

parts of a radio
antenna
speaker
battery

winter sports
hockey
ice skating
bobsledding

Word box:
parts of the leg
winter sports
storms
parts of a radio

19

More Analogies

Directions: Fill in the blanks with words of your own to complete each analogy. One is done for you.

1. Fuse is to firecracker as wick is to candle.
2. Wheel is to steering as brake is to stopping.
3. Scissors are to cut as needle is to sew.
4. Water is to skiing as rink is to skating.
5. Steam shovel is to dig as tractor is to plow.
6. Puck is to hockey as ball is to baseball.
7. Watch is to television as listen is to radio.
8. Geese is to goose as children is to child.
9. Multiply is to multiplication as subtract is to subtraction.
10. Milk is to cow as egg is to chicken.
11. Yellow is to banana as red is to tomato.
12. Fast is to slow as day is to night.
13. Pine is to tree as (varies) is to flower.
14. Zipper is to jacket as button is to shirt.
15. Museum is to painting as library is to book.
16. Petal is to flower as branch is to tree.
17. Cow is to barn as (varies) is to (varies).
18. (varies) is to bedroom as (varies) is to kitchen.
19. Teacher is to student as doctor is to patient.
20. Ice is to cold as (varies) is to (varies).

22

Fact Or Opinion?

Directions: Read the following sentences about states. Beside each one, write whether it is a fact or opinion. One is done for you.

fact 1. Hawaii is the only island state.

opinion 2. The best fishing is in Michigan.

opinion 3. It is easy to find a job in Wyoming.

fact 4. Trenton is the capital of New Jersey.

fact 5. Kentucky is nicknamed the Bluegrass State.

opinion 6. The friendliest people in the United States live in Georgia.

opinion 7. The cleanest beaches are in California.

opinion 8. Summers are most beautiful in Arizona.

fact 9. Only one percent of North Dakota is forest or woodland.

fact 10. New Mexico produces almost half of the nation's uranium.

fact 11. The first shots of the Civil War were fired in South Carolina on April 12, 1861.

fact 12. The varied geographical features of Washington include mountains, desert, a rain forest, and a volcano.

fact 13. In 1959 Alaska and Hawaii became the 49th and 50th states to be admitted to the Union.

fact 14. Wyandotte Cave, one of the largest caves in the United States, is in Indiana.

Directions: Write one fact and one opinion about your own state.

Fact: _answer varies_

Opinion: _answer varies_

23

Fact Or Opinion?

Directions: Read the following very different views of cats. List the facts and opinions in each one.

Cats make the best pets. Domestic or house cats were originally produced by cross-breeding several varieties of wild cats. They were used in ancient Egypt to catch rats and mice, which were overrunning bins of stored grain. Today they are still the most useful domestic animal.

Facts:

1. _Domestic or house cats were produced by cross-breeding wild cats._
2. _They were used in ancient Egypt to catch rats and mice._

Opinions:

1. _Cats make the best pets._
2. _Today they are still the most useful domestic animal._

It is bad luck for a black cat to cross your path. This is one of the many legends about cats. In ancient Egypt, for example, cats were considered sacred, and often were buried with their masters. But during the Middle Ages, cats often were killed for taking part in what people thought were evil deeds. Cats have been thought to bring misfortune.

Facts:

1. _There are many legends about cats._
2. _In ancient Egypt, cats were considered sacred and often buried with their masters._
3. _During the Middle Ages, cats often were killed for taking part in evil deeds._

Opinions:

1. _It is bad luck for a black cat to cross your path._
2. _Cats have been known to bring misfortune._

24

Causes And Their Effects

Directions: Read the following paragraphs. Complete the charts by writing the missing cause (reason) or effect (result).

Club-footed toads are small toads that live in the rain forests of Central and South America. Because they give off a poisonous substance on their skins, other animals cannot eat them.

Cause:
They give off a poisonous substance.

Effect:
Other animals cannot eat them.

Civets (say it SIV-it) are weasel-like animals. The best-known of the civets is the mongoose, which eats rats and snakes. For this reason, it is welcome around homes in its native India.

Cause:
It eats rats and snakes

Effect:
It is welcome around homes in its native India.

Bluebirds can be found in most areas of the United States. Like other members of the thrush family of birds, young bluebirds have speckled breasts. This makes them difficult to see and helps hide them from their enemies. The Pilgrims called them "blue robins" because they are much like the English robin: They are the same size and have the same red breast and friendly song as the English robin.

Cause:
Young bluebirds have speckled breasts.

Effect:
This makes them difficult to see and helps them hide from enemies.

They are much like the English robin. The Pilgrims called them "blue robins."

25

Review

Directions: Follow the directions for each section.

Cross out the word that does not belong. Add a word of your own that does belong.

1. oak ~~wood~~ maple pine _____ (answers vary)
2. roots stem petal ~~air~~ _____
3. paragraph book newspaper magazine _____

Circle the word that completes each analogy.

1. Bear is to woods as fish is to ____ (sea) eggs scales
2. Sit is to chair as ____ is to bed. night bedroom (sleep)
3. ____ is to window as rug is to floor. (curtain) glass open

Write **Fact** or **Opinion** to describe each sentence.

fact 1. Australia is the smallest continent.

opinion 2. The Australians are the friendliest people in the world.

fact 3. You will see kangaroos and koala bears in Australia.

Directions: Write the letter of the effect (right column) next to its cause (left column).

_d_ As fuel supplies dwindle a. we had few flowers this Spring.

_c_ Because she wants to help sick people b. Jacob wouldn't eat his broccoli.

_e_ It had stormed the night before c. Mary plans to go to medical school.

_b_ Because he doesn't like vegetables d. prices will rise.

_a_ Because the squirrels are our tulip bulbs e. and many large trees were toppled.

26

Using A Newspaper Index

Newspapers give you all kinds of information. They will tell you about the national and local news, the weather, and sports. You will also find opinions, feature stories, advice columns, comics, entertainment, recipes, advertisements, and more. An index of the newspaper usually appears on the front page.

Directions: Use the newspaper index to answer the following questions. Give the section where you would look and the page numbers where it appears.

Business 8	Local News ..5-7
Classified Ads ..18-19	National News ..1-4
Comics 20	Radio-TV 17
Editorials 9	Sports 11-13
Entertainment 14-16	Weather 10

1. Where would you look for results of last night's basketball games?
Sports, pages 11-13.

2. Where would you find your favorite cartoon strip? _Comics, 20_

3. Where would you find the editor's opinion of upcoming elections?
Editorials, 9

4. Where would you look to locate a used bicycle to buy? _Classified Ads, 18-19._

5. Where would you find out if you need to wear your raincoat tomorrow?
Weather, 10

6. Where would you find the listing of tonight's TV shows? _TV/Radio, 17_

7. Explain which would be first, a story about the President's trip to Europe or a review of the movie "Teenage Mutant Ninja Turtles."
The President's trip would be first because it's national news, which is on pages 1-4.

27

Classified Ads

An advertisement tells about a product or service for sale.

Directions: Read the following advertisements, then answer the questions.

1.
Yard Work Breaking Your Back?
Give Mike and Jane a Crack
Mowing, raking, trash hauled.
References provided.
Call 572-9581

2.
Pet Sitter
Going on vacation?
Away for the weekend?
I am 14 years old and have experience caring for dogs and cats.
Your home or mine.
Excellent references.
Call Sally Trent
Phone: 999-8250

3.
Singing Lessons for All Ages!
Be popular at parties!
Fulfill your dreams!
20 years coaching experience.
Madame Rinaud ...
Coach to the Stars!
787-5331

1. What is promised from the third ad? Is it fact or opinion?
You will be popular and fulfill your dreams Opinion

2. What fact is offered in the third ad?
20 years coaching experience.

3. Give an example of a slogan, or easy-to-remember phrase, that appears in one of the ads.
Yard work breaking your back? Give Mike and Jane a crack!

4. Which ad gives the most facts?
second

5. Which ad is based mostly on opinion?
third

28

77

What's On TV?

Directions: Use the newspaper program listing below to answer the questions.

Evening	
6:00	[3] **Let's Talk!** Guest: Animal expert Jim Porter.
	[5] **Cartoons**
	[8] **News**
	[9] **News**
7:00	[3] **Farm Report**
	[5] **Movie.** "A Laugh a Minute" (1955) James Rayburn. Comedy about a boy who wants to join the circus.
	[8] **Spin for Dollars!**
	[9] **Cooking with Cathy.** Tonight: Chicken with mushrooms.
7:30	[3] **Double Trouble** (comedy). The twins disrupt the high school dance.
	[8] **Wall Street Today:** Stock Market Report
8:00	[3] **NBA Basketball.** Teams to be announced
	[8] **News Special.** "Saving Our Waterways: Pollution in the Mississippi."
	[9] **Movie. At Day's End"** (1981) Michael Collier, Julie Romer. Drama set in World War II.

1. What two stations have the news at 6:00?

8 and 9

2. What time would you turn on the television to watch a funny movie? What channel?

7:00, channel 5

3. What might you turn on if you are a sports fan? What time and channel?

NBA Basketball. 8:00, ch. 3

4. Which show title sounds like it could be a game show?

Spin for Dollars!

5. 1) What show might you want to watch if you are interested in helping the environment?

Saving Our Waterways: Pollution in the Mississippi

2) What time and channel?

8:00, channel 8

Copyright © 1991 American Education Publishing Co.

29

Reading A Map

Directions: Use the map of Columbus, Ohio, to answer the questions.

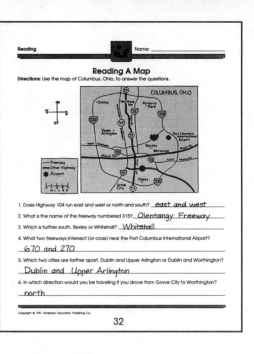

1. Does Highway 104 run east and west or north and south? _east and west_

2. What is the name of the freeway numbered 315? _Olentangy Freeway_

3. Which is south, Bexley or Whitehall? _Whitehall_

4. What two freeways intersect (or cross) near the Port Columbus International Airport?

670 and 270

5. Which two cities are farther apart, Dublin and Upper Arlington or Dublin and Worthington?

Dublin and Upper Arlington

6. In which direction would you be traveling if you drove from Grove City to Worthington?

north

Copyright © 1991 American Education Publishing Co.

32

Medicine Labels

Directions: Read the label from a medicine bottle, then answer the questions.

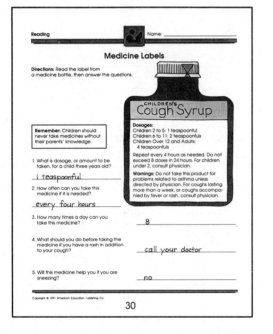

CHILDREN'S **Cough Syrup**

Remember: Children should never take medicines without their parents' knowledge.

Dosages:
Children 2 to 5: 1 teaspoonful
Children 6 to 11: 2 teaspoonfuls
Children Over 12 and Adults: 4 teaspoonfuls

Repeat every 4 hours as needed. Do not exceed 8 doses in 24 hours. For children under 2, consult physician.

Warnings: Do not take this product for problems related to asthma unless directed by physician. For coughs lasting more than a week, or coughs accompanied by fever or rash, consult physician.

1. What is dosage, or amount to be taken, for a child three years old?

1 teaspoonful

2. How often can you take this medicine if it is needed?

every four hours

3. How many times a day can you take this medicine?

_8_

4. What should you do before taking the medicine if you have a rash in addition to your cough?

call your doctor

5. Will this medicine help you if you are sneezing?

_no_

Copyright © 1991 American Education Publishing Co.

30

Skimming And Scanning

In skimming, look for headings and key words to give you an overall idea of what you are reading.

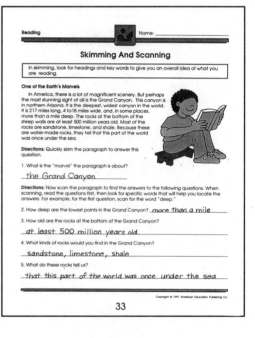

One of the Earth's Marvels

In America, there is a lot of magnificent scenery. But perhaps the most stunning sight of all is the Grand Canyon. This canyon is in northern Arizona. It is the deepest, widest canyon in the world. It is 217 miles long, 4 to 18 miles wide, and, in some places, more than a mile deep. The rocks at the bottom of the steep walls are at least 500 million years old. Most of the rocks are sandstone, limestone, and shale. Because these are water-made rocks, they tell us that this part of the world was once under the sea.

Directions: Quickly skim the paragraph to answer this question.

1. What is the "marvel" the paragraph is about?

the Grand Canyon

Directions: Now scan the paragraph to find the answers to the following questions. When scanning, read the questions first, then look for specific words that will help you locate the answers. For example, for the first question, scan for the word "deep."

2. How deep are the lowest points in the Grand Canyon? _more than a mile_

3. How old are the rocks at the bottom of the Grand Canyon?

at least 500 million years old

4. What kinds of rocks would you find in the Grand Canyon?

sandstone, limestone, shale

5. What do these rocks tell us?

that this part of the world was once under the sea

Copyright © 1991 American Education Publishing Co.

33

Reading A Map

Maps give you information about places. Good maps include such features as a legend, compass, scale of distance, latitude/longitude lines, and color key. If you understand them, you can use and understand any map.

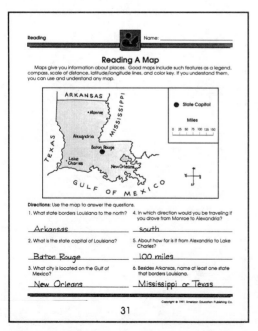

• **State Capitol**

Miles
0 25 50 75 100 125 150

Directions: Use the map to answer the questions.

1. What state borders Louisiana to the north?

Arkansas

2. What is the state capital of Louisiana?

Baton Rouge

3. What city is located on the Gulf of Mexico?

New Orleans

4. In which direction would you be traveling if you drove from Monroe to Alexandria?

south

5. About how far is it from Alexandria to Lake Charles?

100 miles

6. Besides Arkansas, name at least one state that borders Louisiana.

Mississippi or Texas

Copyright © 1991 American Education Publishing Co.

31

Review

Road Closing Announced

Beginning Monday, drivers in northern Columbus may be facing more traffic jams. The Ohio Department of Transportation has announced that State Route 315 will be closed between Interstates 270 and 670 for repairs. The closing will be in effect for the next three weeks. For alternate routes, drivers can use State Route 23 or Interstate 71.

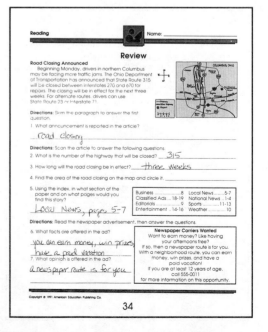

Directions: Skim the paragraph to answer the first question.

1. What announcement is reported in the article?

road closing

Directions: Scan the article to answer the following questions.

2. What is the number of the highway that will be closed? _315_

3. How long will the road closing be in effect? _three weeks_

4. Find the area of the road closing on the map and circle it.

5. Using the index, in what section of the paper and on what pages would you find this story?

Local News, pages 5-7

Business	8	Local News	5-7
Classified Ads	18-19	National News	1-4
Editorials	9	Sports	11-13
Entertainment	14-16	Weather	10

Directions: Read the newspaper advertisement, then answer the questions.

6. What facts are offered in the ad?

you can earn money, win prizes, have a paid vacation

7. What opinion is offered in the ad?

a newspaper route is for you

Newspaper Carriers Wanted
Want to earn money? Like having your afternoons free? If so, a newspaper route is for you. With a neighborhood route, you can earn money, win prizes, and have a paid vacation! If you are at least 12 years of age, call 555-0011 for more information on this opportunity.

Copyright © 1991 American Education Publishing Co.

34

The Coldest Continent

Antarctica

Antarctica, which lies on the South Pole, is the coldest continent. It is without sunlight for months at a time. Even when the sun does shine there, its angle is so slanted that the land receives little warmth. Temperatures often drop to 100 degrees below zero, and a fierce wind blows almost endlessly. Most of the land is covered by snow heaped thousands of feet deep. The snow is so heavy and tightly packed that it forms a great ice cap covering more than 95 percent of the continent.

It is no wonder that there are no towns or cities in Antarctica. There is no permanent population at all, only small scientific research stations. Many teams of explorers and scientists have braved the freezing cold since Antarctica was first spotted in 1820. Some have died in their efforts, but a great deal of information has been learned about the continent.

From fossils, pieces of coal, and bone samples, we know that Antarctica was not always an ice-covered land. Scientists believe that 200 million years ago it was connected to southern Africa, South America, Australia, and India. Forests grew in warm swamps, and insects and reptiles thrived there. Today, there are animals that live in and around the waters that border the continent. In fact, the waters surrounding Antarctica hold more life than oceans in warmer areas of the world.

Directions: Answer these questions about Antarctica.

1. Where is Antarctica? _on the South Pole_

2. How much of the continent is covered by an ice cap? _more than 95 percent_

3. When was Antarctica first sighted by explorers? _1820_

4. What things have provided clues that Antarctica was not always an ice-covered land?
fossils, coal, bones

35

Exploring The Frozen Continent

By the mid-1800s, most of the seals of Antarctica had been killed off. The seal hunters no longer sailed the icy waters. The explorers who next took an interest in Antarctica were scientists. Of these, one who took the most daring chances and made the most amazing discoveries was British Captain James Clark Ross.

Ross first made a name for himself sailing to the north. In 1831 he discovered the North Magnetic Pole — one of two places on earth toward which a compass needle points. In 1840, Ross set out to find the South Magnetic Pole. He made many marvelous discoveries, including the Ross Sea, a great open sea beyond the ice packs that stopped other explorers, and the Ross Ice Shelf, a great floating sheet of ice bigger than all of France!

The next man to make his mark exploring Antarctica was the British explorer Robert Falcon Scott. Scott set out in 1902 to find the South Pole. He and his team suffered greatly, but they were able to make it a third of the way to the pole. Back in England, Scott was a great hero. In 1910, he again attempted to become the first man to reach the South Pole. But this time had competition: An explorer from Norway, Roald Amundsen, was also leading a team to the South Pole.

It was a brutal race. Both teams faced many hardships, but they pressed on. Finally, on December 14, 1911, Amundsen became the first man ever to reach the South Pole. Scott arrived on January 17, 1912. He was bitterly disappointed at not being first. The trip back was even more horrible. Not one of the five men in the Scott expedition survived.

Directions: Answer these questions about explorers.

1. After the seal hunters, who were the next group of explorers interested in Antarctica?
Scientists

2. Name two of the great discoveries made by James Ross.
1) _The Ross Sea_   2) _The Ross Ice Shelf_

3. What big discovery did James Ross make before ever sailing to Antarctica?
The north magnetic pole

4. How close did Scott and his team come to finding the South Pole in 1902?
A third of the way

5. Who was the first man to reach the South Pole? _Roald Amundsen_

38

The Other Pole

The Arctic Circle

On the other side of the world from Antarctica, at the northernmost part of the world, is another icy land. This is the Arctic Circle. It includes the North Pole itself, the northern fringes of three continents — Europe, Asia, and North America (including the state of Alaska) — as well as Greenland and other islands.

The seasons are opposite on the two ends of the world. When it is summer in Antarctica, it is winter in the Arctic Circle. In both places, there are very long periods of sunlight in summer and very long nights in the winter. On the poles themselves, there are six full months of sunlight and six full months of darkness each year.

Compared to Antarctica, the summers are surprisingly mild in some areas of the Arctic Circle. Much of the snow cover may melt, and temperatures often reach 50 degrees in July. But neither of the polar regions can support plant life. Antarctica is covered with water — frozen water, of course — so nothing can grow there. Plant growth is limited in the polar regions not only by the cold, but also by wind, lack of water, and the long winter darkness.

In the Far North, willow trees do grow, but only to be a few inches high! The annual rings — the circles within the trunk of a tree that show its age and how fast it grows — in these trees are so narrow that you need a microscope to see them.

A permanently frozen layer of soil, called "permafrost," keeps roots from growing deep enough into the ground to anchor a plant. Even if a plant could survive the cold temperatures, it could not grow roots deep enough or strong enough to allow the plant to get very big.

Directions: Answer these questions about the Arctic Circle.

1. What three continents have land included in the Arctic Circle?
a. _Europe_ b. _Asia_ c. _North America_

2. Is the Arctic Circle generally warmer or colder than Antarctica? _warmer_

3. What are the annual rings of a tree? _the circles in the trunk of the tree that tell how old it is and how fast it is growing_

4. What is "permafrost"? _a permanently frozen layer of soil_

36

Polar Bears

There are animals that are able to survive the cold weather and difficult conditions of the snow and ice fields in the polar regions. One of the best known is the polar bear of the North Pole.

Polar bears live on the land and the sea. They may drift hundreds of miles from land on huge sheets of floating ice. They use their great paws to paddle the ice along. Polar bears are excellent swimmers, too. They can cross great distances of open water. While in the sea, they feed mostly on fish and seals.

On the land, these huge animals, which measure ten feet long and weigh about 1000 pounds, can run 25 miles an hour. Surprisingly, polar bears live as plant eaters rather than hunters while on land. Unlike many kinds of bears, polar bears do not hibernate. They are active the whole year long.

Baby polar bears are born during the winter. They are pink and almost hairless. These helpless cubs weigh only two pounds — less than one-third the size of most human infants. The mother rears her young in dens dug in snow banks. By the time they are ten weeks old, polar bear cubs are about the size of puppies and have enough white fur to protect them in the open air. The mother gives her cubs swimming, hunting, and fishing lessons. But by the time autumn comes, the cubs are left to survive on their own.

Directions: Answer these questions about polar bears.

Circle **Yes** or **No**

1. Polar Bears can live on the land and on the sea.   (Yes) No
2. Polar Bears are excellent swimmers.   (Yes) No
3. Polar Bears hibernate in the winter.   Yes (No)
4. A newborn polar bear weighs more than a newborn human baby.   Yes (No)
5. Mother polar bears raise their babies in caves.   Yes (No)
6. Father bears give the cubs swimming lessons.   Yes (No)

39

Blazing The Polar Trail

Antarctica, the last continent to be discovered, was not sighted until the early nineteenth century. Since then, many brave explorers and adventurers have sailed south to conquer the icy land. Their achievements once gained as much attention as those of the first astronauts.

Long before the continent was first spotted, the ancient Greeks had guessed that there was a continent at the bottom of the world. Over the centuries, legends of the undiscovered land spread. Some of the world's greatest seamen tried to find it, including Captain James Cook in 1772.

Cook was the first to sail all the way to the solid field of ice that surrounds Antarctica every winter. In fact, he sailed all the way around the continent but never saw it. Cook went farther south than anyone had ever gone. His record lasted fifty years.

Forty years after Cook, a new kind of seaman sailed the icy waters. They were the hunters of seals and whales. Sailing through unknown waters in search of seals, these men became explorers as well as hunters. It is believed that the first person to sight Antarctica was one of these hunters, a 21-year-old American named Nathaniel Brown Palmer. The year was 1820.

Directions: Answer these questions about Antarctica.

Check √

1. The main idea is:

☐ Antarctica was not sighted until the early nineteenth century.

☑ Many brave explorers and adventurers have sailed south to conquer the icy land.

Write

2. Who was the first person to sail to the ice field that surrounds Antarctica?
Captain James Cook

3. How long did his record for sailing the farthest south stand? _fifty years_

4. Who is thought to be the first man to sight Antarctica? _Nathanial Brown Palmer_

5. What was his profession? _seal hunter_

37

Seals

Seals are **aquatic** mammals that have kept a liking for land. Some seals stay in the sea for weeks or months at a time, even sleeping in the water. But all seals need the land at some time. To avoid people and other animals, they pick **secluded** spots to come onto the land.

The 31 different kinds of seals belong to a group of animals that is often called "pinnipeds," or fin-footed. Their fins, or flippers, make them very good swimmers and divers. Their nostrils close tightly when they dive. They have been know to stay **submerged** for as long as a half-hour at a time!

Seals are warm-blooded animals that can adjust to various temperatures. They live in both **temperate** and cold climates. Besides their fur, seals have a thick layer of fat called "blubber" to help protect them against the cold. It is harder for seals to cool themselves in hot weather than to warm themselves in cold weather. They sometimes can become so overheated that they die.

Directions: Answer these questions about seals.

Check √

1. Based on the other words in the sentence, what is the correct definition for "aquatic"?
☐ living on the land
☑ living on or in the sea
☐ living in large groups

2. Based on the other words in the sentence, what is the correct definition for "secluded"?
☐ rocky
☑ private or hidden
☐ near other animals

3. Based on the other words in the sentence, what is the correct definition for "submerged"?
☑ under the water
☐ on top of the water
☐ in groups

4. Based on the other word in the sentence, what is the correct definition for "temperate"?
☐ rainy
☐ measured on a thermometer
☑ warm

40

79

The Walrus

Walruses are actually a kind of seal that live only in the Arctic Circle. They have two huge upper teeth, or tusks, they use to pull themselves out of the water or to move over the rocks on land. They also use them to dig clams, one of their favorite foods, from the bottom of the sea. In an adult male walrus, the tusks may be three and a half feet long!

Walruses have unusual faces. Besides their long tusks, they have big, bushy mustaches made up of hundreds of movable, stiff bristles. They help the walrus to push food into his mouth. Also, except for a small wrinkle in the skin, walruses have no outer ears.

Like the seal, the walrus uses his flippers to help him swim. His front flippers serve as paddles, and he swings the back of his huge body from side to side. A walrus looks awkward using his flippers to walk on land, but don't be fooled! A walrus can run as fast as a man.

Baby walruses are born in the early spring. They never leave their mothers until they are two years old. There is a good reason for this — they must grow little tusks, at least three or four inches long, before they can catch their own food from the bottom of the sea. Until then, they must stay close to their mothers to eat. A young walrus that is tired from swimming will climb onto his mother's back for a ride, holding onto her with his front flippers.

Directions: Answers these questions about walruses.

1. The walrus is a type of seal found only <u>in the Arctic Circle</u>

2. List two ways the walrus uses his tusks.

  1) <u>for pulling himself out of water and over rocks</u>

  2) <u>for digging food from the bottom of the sea</u>

Directions: Circle **Yes** or **No**

3. A walrus cannot move quickly on land.   Yes (No)

4. A baby walrus must stay very close to its mother until it is two years old.   (Yes) No

41

Review

Penguins are among the best-liked animals in the world. People are amused by their funny duck-like waddle and their appearance of wearing little tuxedos. But the penguin is a much misunderstood animal. There may be more wrong ideas about penguins than any other animal.

For example, many people are surprised to learn that penguins are really birds. Penguins do not fly, but they do have feathers, and only birds have feathers. Also, like other birds, penguins build nests and their young are hatched from eggs. Because of their unusual looks, though, you would never confuse them with any other bird!

Penguins are also thought of as symbols of the polar regions. But no penguins have ever lived north of the equator, so you would not find a penguin at the North Pole. And penguins don't live at the South Pole, either. Just two of the seventeen **species** of penguin spend all of their lives on the frozen continent of Antarctica. You would be just as likely to see a penguin living on an island in a warm climate as in a cold area.

Directions: Answer these questions about penguins.

Check √

1. The main idea is:
- ☐ Penguins are among the best-liked animals in the world.
- ☑ The penguin is a much misunderstood animal.

2. Penguins live
- ☐ only at the North Pole
- ☐ only at the South Pole
- ☑ only south of the equator

3. Based on the other words in the sentence, what is the correct definition of the word "species"?
- ☐ number
- ☐ bird
- ☑ a distinct kind

Write

4. List three ways penguins are like other birds.

  1) <u>they have feathers</u>

  2) <u>they build nests</u>

  3) <u>their young are hatched from eggs</u>

42

The Earliest Forms Of Printing

When people talk about printing, they usually mean making exact copies of an original document, such as a paper or even an entire book. The inventions that have allowed us to do this are some of the most important developments in the history of man. Look around you. How many examples can you find of things that have been printed? Can you imagine life without it?

The oldest known example of a printed book was made in China in 848. A man named Wang Chieh made the book by carving each page by hand onto a block of wood. He then put ink on the wood and pressed it to a piece of paper. This idea of printing with wood blocks spread to Europe. The letters in these block books were made to look handwritten.

In about 1440, a German goldsmith named Johann Gutenberg developed the idea of movable type. This meant that letters were made separately. The letters could be fastened together to make words and sentences. They were made out of metal so they could be used again and again. This wonderful invention made it possible to have more and cheaper reading material.

Gutenberg had other ideas that were important to printing. He developed a kind of ink that would stick to the new metal type. Gutenberg's ideas were so successful that the process of printing went almost unchanged for more than 300 years.

Directions: Answer these questions about printing.

1. In what country was the oldest known printed book made? <u>China</u>

2. What is "movable type"? <u>letters made separately that could be used again and again</u>

3. What was the name of the man who developed the idea of movable type?
<u>Johann Gutenberg</u>

4. What was another important invention of Gutenberg? <u>ink that would stick to metal type</u>

5. Who made the first printed book? <u>Wang Chieh</u>

43

Read All About It!

Newspapers. They keep us informed about what is going on in the world. They entertain, educate, and examine the events of the day. For hundreds of years, newspapers have been read by millions of people worldwide. Newspapers are part of their daily lives.

Newspapers are published at various intervals, but they usually come out daily or weekly. Of the nearly 60,000 newspapers being published around the world, about 2600 are published in the United States. More than half — about 1800 — of them are dailies.

Some newspapers have a lot of subscribers — people who pay to have each edition delivered to them. For example, The Wall Street Journal and USA Today each have about two million subscribers. But there are many, many more newspapers with only a few thousand subscribers. These include small-town weeklies and special-interest papers such as those written for people who enjoy the same hobby.

Newspapers provide a service to the community by providing information at little cost. But they also are businesses and so they need to make money. They can keep the cost to the reader low and still stay in business by selling space to businesses and individuals who want to advertise products or services. In most newspapers, between one-third and two-thirds of the paper is taken up by advertising.

Directions: Answer these questions about newspapers.

1. How many newspapers are thought to be published worldwide? <u>60,000</u>

2. What are "subscribers"? <u>people who pay to have each edition delivered to them</u>

3. At what intervals are most newspapers published? <u>daily or weekly</u>

4. What do newspapers do to keep the cost to the reader low but still make money?

<u>sell advertising space</u>

44

The First Newspapers

The earliest newspapers were probably handwritten notices posted to be read by the public. But the first true newspaper was a weekly newspaper started in Germany in 1609. It was called the Strassburg Relation. The Germans were pioneers in newspaper publishing. (Johann Gutenberg, the man who developed the idea of movable type, was from Germany.)

One of the first English-language newspapers, The London Gazette, was printed in England in 1665. "Gazette" is an old English word that means "official publication." Many newspapers today still use the word gazette in their names.

In America, several papers were started during the colonial days. The first successful one, The Boston News-Letter, began printing in 1704. It was very small — about the size of a sheet of notebook paper with printing on both sides.

An important date in newspaper publishing was 1833. In that year, The New York Sun became the first penny newspaper. They actually did cost only a penny. The penny newspapers were similar to today's papers. They printed news while it was still new. They also were the first to print advertisements and to sell papers in newsstands. And penny newspapers were the first to be delivered to homes.

Directions: Answer these questions about early newspapers.

1. In what year was the first true newspaper printed? <u>1609</u>

2. What was the name of the first successful newspaper in America?

<u>The Boston News-Letter</u>

3. Why was 1833 important in newspaper publishing? <u>The New York Sun became the first penny newspaper</u>

4. List four ways the penny newspapers were like the newspapers of today?

  1) <u>they printed the news while it was new</u>   3) <u>they were sold in newsstands</u>

  2) <u>they sold advertisements</u>   4) <u>they were delivered to homes</u>

45

Freedom Of The Press

In the United States, we have certain rights or freedoms that are **guaranteed** to us by the Constitution. Freedom of the press is one of the **privileges** provided for in the Bill of Rights. Press originally referred to newspapers, magazines, books, pamphlets — anything printed on a printing press. Today, television, movies, and radio are also included.

Freedom of the press is the right to gather and publish information or opinions without the control of the government. Before the Bill of Rights, the government could stop newspapers from writing stories it didn't like or information it didn't want the public to know. This form of **censorship** is still practiced in some countries.

An important test of freedom of the press occurred in 1735. A man named John Peter Zenger, a newspaper publisher in New York, was arrested and put in jail for **criticizing** the colonial government. At his trial, his lawyer did not deny that Zenger printed the material. But he challenged the jury to decide whether what Zenger printed was true. The jury believed that it was and found Zenger not guilty. This was the first test of the right of the press to print the truth, even if the government didn't like it.

Directions: Answer these questions about freedom of the press.

Check √

1. Based on the other words in the sentence, what is the correct definition for "guaranteed"?
- ☐ written
- ☑ pledged or promised
- ☐ provide

2. Based on the other words in the sentence, what is the correct definition for "privilege"?
- ☑ right
- ☐ law
- ☐ anything printed

3. Based on the other words in the sentence, what is the correct definition for "censorship"?
- ☐ laws
- ☐ writing
- ☑ not allowing certain information to be published

4. Based on the other words in the sentence, what is the correct definition for "criticizing"?
- ☑ disapproving of
- ☐ agreeing with
- ☐ talking about

46

Jobs At A Newspaper

It takes a whole army of people to put out one of the big daily newspapers. There are three separate departments needed to make a newspaper operate smoothly: editorial, mechanical, and business.

The editorial department is the one most people think about first. That is the news-gathering part of the newspaper. The most familiar job in this department is that of the reporter — the person who gets the information for a story and writes it. A photographer takes the pictures to go with the reporter's story.

Editors are the decision makers. There are many editors at a newspaper to do such jobs as assigning the stories to reporters, reading the stories to make sure they are correct, and deciding where the stories should appear in the paper. The most important stories go on the front page. There are also picture editors who choose which pictures will appear in the paper. Other jobs in the editorial department include artists, copy editors, proofreaders, and cartoonists.

The biggest job in the mechanical department is printing the paper. Most larger newspapers have their own printing presses. Some small papers send their work to outside printing shops. After an issue, or edition, is printed, it is ready to be sold or "circulated" to the public.

The circulation of the paper is one of the jobs of the business department. This department also sells the advertising space. This is very important for newspapers. Many papers make more money selling advertising space than selling newspapers. The business department also takes care of normal business jobs, such as paying the bills and keeping records.

Directions: Answer these questions about newspaper jobs.

1. Name the three main departments at a newspaper.
1) _editorial_   2) _mechanical_   3) _business_

2. Who are the people who get the information for a story and write it? _reporters_

3. Who are the decision-makers at a newspaper? _editors_

4. What is the biggest job for the mechanical department? _printing the paper_

The Story Of A Story

Here is an example of how a story gets into the newspaper:

Let's imagine that a city bus has turned over in a ditch, injuring some of the passengers. An **eyewitness** calls the newspaper. The editor assigns a reporter to go to the scene. The reporter talks to the passengers. She finds out what they saw and how they feel, writing down their comments in a notebook. At the same time, a photographer is busy taking pictures.

If there isn't time for the reporter to go back to the office, she telephones it in. A copytaker types the story onto a computer as the reporter **dictates** it. (Many newspapers today have word processors on which the reporter can write the story on the spot, and then send it back to the office over the telephone lines.) Next an editor will read the story, checking the facts and making sure there are no grammar or spelling mistakes. Meanwhile, the photographer's film is developed and a picture is chosen. It is sent to the processing department.

The story is set in print. On most newspapers today, this can be done with a computer. The computer makes sets of columns of type, which are pasted onto a sheet of paper exactly the same size as a newspaper page. A **proofreader** checks the story for mistakes. The newspaper is ready for printing. The presses begin to run. Miles of paper are turned into thousands of printed, cut, and folded newspapers. They are counted and put into bundles, and placed in waiting trucks. Within only a few hours, people can read about the bus accident in their daily newspaper.

Directions: Answer these questions about news stories.

Check √
1. Based on the other words in the sentence, what is the correct definition for "eyewitness"?
☐ a reporter
☑ a person who saw what happened
☐ a lawyer

2. Based on the other words in the sentence, what is the correct definition for "dictates"?
☐ photographs
☐ writes
☑ reads story word for word

3. Based on the other words in the sentence, what is the correct definition for "proofreader"?
☑ person who reads for mistakes
☐ teacher
☐ printer

News Services

Most people who read daily newspapers expect to see news from all over the world. Some newspapers do have offices or reporters in Washington, D.C., and other major cities around the world. But most newspapers rely on news services for international news. These are organizations that gather and sell news to papers and even radio and television stations. They are sometimes referred to as "wire services" because they would send stories over telegraph or teletype lines, or "wires."

The two largest news services are the Associated Press and United Press International. Stories sent by these services have their initials — AP or UPI — at the beginning. All large American newspapers are members of either the AP or UPI services.

The gathering of news from around the world has been greatly speeded up by the inventions of the telegraph, telephone, cable, radio, teletype and facsimile machines. Today, stories and even pictures can be sent around the world in a matter of minutes.

Directions: Answer these questions about news services.

1. What is another name for news service organizations? _wire services_

2. List the two largest news service organizations.
1) _the Associated Press_
2) _United Press International_

3. List three inventions that have speeded up the worldwide gathering of news.
1) _____
2) _____
3) _____
telephone, telegraph, cable, radio, teletype, facsimile machines are all correct answers for number 3.

81

Review

Samuel Langhorne Clemens was born in Florida, Missouri, in 1835. In his lifetime, he gained worldwide fame as a writer, lecturer, and humorist.

Clemens first worked for a printer when he was only 12 years old. Soon after that he worked on his brother's newspaper.

Clemens traveled a lot and worked as a printer in New York, Philadelphia, St. Louis, and Cincinnati. On a trip to New Orleans in 1857, he learned the difficult art of steamboat piloting. Clemens loved this and later used it as a background for some of his books, including Life on the Mississippi.

A few years later, Clemens went to Nevada with his brother and tried goldmining. When this proved unsuccessful, he went back to writing for newspapers. At first he signed his humorous pieces with the name "Josh." But in 1863 he began signing them Mark Twain. The words "mark twain" are used by river pilots to mean "two fathoms (12 feet) deep" — safe water for steamboats. From then on, Clemens used this now-famous **pseudonym** for all of his writing.

As Mark Twain, he began to receive attention from all over the world. His best-known works include Tom Sawyer and The Adventures of Huckleberry Finn. These are still two of the most beloved books about boyhood.

Directions: Answer these questions about Samuel Clemens.

Write
1. Under what name did Samuel Clemens write his books? _Mark Twain_

2. What do the words "mark twain" really mean? _two fathoms deep_

3. Besides author, list two other jobs held by Mark Twain. _printer, reporter, steamboat pilot, goldminer, lecturer_
1) _____   2) _____

4. List two of the best-known books written by Mark Twain.
1) _Tom Sawyer_   2) _The Adventures of Huckleberry Finn_

Check √
5. Based on the other words in the sentence, what is the correct definition for "pseudonym"?
☐ book title
☑ a made-up name used by an author
☐ a humorous article

The Desert

Deserts are found where there is little rainfall, or where the rainfall for a whole year falls in only a few weeks' time. Ten inches of rain may be enough for many plants to survive if the rain is spread out throughout the year. But if the ten inches falls during one or two months and the rest of the year is dry, a desert may form.

When many people think of deserts, they think of long stretches of sand. Sand begins as tiny pieces of rock that get smaller and smaller as wind and weather wear them down. Sand dunes, or hills of drifting sand, are made as winds move the sand over the desert. Grain by grain, the dune grows over the years, always shifting with the winds and changing its shape. Most dunes are only a few feet tall, but they can grow to be several hundred feet high.

There is, however, much more to a desert than sand. In the deserts of the southwestern United States, cliffs and canyons were formed from thick mud that once lay beneath a sea more than a hundred million years ago. Over the centuries, the water drained away. Wind, sand, rain, heat, and cold all carved away at the remaining rocks. The faces of the desert mountains are always changing — very, very slowly — as these forces of nature continue to work on the rock.

Most deserts have surprising varieties of life. There are plants, animals, and insects that have adapted to life in the desert. During the heat of the day, a visitor may see very few signs of living things. But as the air begins to cool in the evening, the desert comes to life. As the sun begins to rise again in the sky, the desert is once again quiet and lonely.

Directions: Answer these questions about deserts.

Circle **Yes** or **No**
1. Deserts are found where there is little rainfall or where the rainfall for a whole year falls in only a few weeks.   (Yes)   No

2. Sand begins as tiny pieces of rock that get smaller and smaller as wind and weather wear them down.   (Yes)   No

3. Sand dunes were formed from thick mud that once lay beneath a sea more than a hundred million years ago.   Yes   (No)

4. The faces of the desert mountains can never change.   Yes   (No)

5. Most deserts have surprising varieties of life.   (Yes)   No

---

Desert Weather

One definition of a desert is an area that has, on the average, less than ten inches of rain a year. Many deserts have far less than that. Death Valley in the United States, for example, receives less than two inches of rain each year. The driest of all is the Atacama Desert in Chile, where no rain at all has ever been known to fall!

Some deserts have a regular rainy season each year, but usually desert rainfall is totally unpredictable. An area may have no rainfall for many years, and then suddenly be flooded by rain. Sometimes a passing cloud may look like it will send relief to the waiting land, but only a "ghost rain" falls. This means that the hot, dry air dries up the raindrops long before they ever reach the ground.

The temperatures in the desert range greatly. The daytime temperatures in the desert frequently top 120 degrees. In Death Valley, they have been know to reach 190 degrees! In most parts of the world, the moisture in the air works like a blanket to hold the heat of the day close to the earth at night. But, because it has no moisture, the desert has no such blanket. This means that the nighttime temperatures are very chilly. Temperatures have been known to drop by fifty or even one hundred degrees at night.

Directions: Answer these questions about desert weather.

1. How much rainfall in a year is used in one definition of desert? _less than ten inches_

2. What is the driest desert in the world? _the Atacama Desert in Chile_

3. What is a "ghost rain"? _hot, dry air dries up raindrops from a rain shower before they can reach the earth_

4. In other parts of the world, what works as a "blanket" to hold the heat of the day close to the earth at night? _moisture in the air_

5. Are the nights in the deserts hot or cold? _cold_

Lakes In The Desert?

A few deserts have small permanent lakes. While they may be a welcome sight in the desert, the water in them is not fit for drinking. These lakes are salt lakes. Rains from nearby higher land keep these lakes supplied with water. But, because the lakes are blocked in with nowhere to drain, over the years mineral salts collect there and build up to a high level.

Most desert lakes are only temporary. The occasional rains may fill them to depths of several feet, but in a matter of weeks or months all of the water has been dried up by the heat and sun. The dried lake beds that remain are called playas. Some playas are simply areas of sun-baked mud; others are covered with a sparkling layer of salt.

Perhaps the most unusual desert lake is in central Australia. It is called Lake Eyre. It is a huge lake — nearly 3,600 square miles in area — but it is almost totally dry most of the time. Since it was discovered in 1840, it has been filled only two times. Both times the lake completely dried up within a few years.

Directions: Answer these questions about desert lakes.

1. Why is the water in a desert lake not fit for drinking? _it is salt water_

2. Why are the lakes in the desert salt lakes? _because mineral salts_
collect there

3. What is a "playa"? _a dry lake bed_

4. Name the desert lake in central Australia. _Lake Eyre_

5. How big is this desert lake? _3,600 square miles_

53

Desert Plants

Desert plants have special features, or adaptations, that allow them to **survive** the harsh conditions of the desert. A cactus stores water in its tissues at times of rain. It then can use this supply over a long dry season. The tiny needles on some kinds of **cacti** may number in the tens of thousands. These sharp thorns protect the cactus. They also form tiny shadows in the sunlight that help keep the plant from getting too hot.

Other plants are able to live by dropping their leaves. This cuts down on the **evaporation** of their water supply in the hot sun. Still other plants survive as seeds, protected from the sun and heat by tough seed coats. When it rains, the seeds **sprout** quickly, bloom, and produce more seeds that can **withstand** long dry spells.

Some plants spread their roots close to the earth's surface to quickly gather water when it does rain. Other plants, such as the mesquite (say it mes-KEET), have roots that grow fifty or sixty feet below the earth's surface to reach underground water supplies.

Directions: Answer these questions about desert plants.

Check √

1. Based on the other words in the sentence, what is the correct definition for "survive"?
- ☑ continue to live
- ☐ die
- ☐ flower

2. Based on the other words in the sentence, what is the correct definition of "cacti"?
- ☐ kind of leaf
- ☑ more than one cactus
- ☐ roots

3. Based on the other words in the sentence, what is the correct definition of "evaporation"?
- ☑ water loss from heat
- ☐ increased
- ☐ boiling

4. Based on the other words in the sentence, what is the correct definition of "sprout"?
- ☐ die
- ☑ begin to grow
- ☐ flower

5. Based on the other words in the sentence, what is the correct definition of "withstand"?
- ☑ put up with
- ☐ stand up
- ☐ take from

54

The Cactus Family

Cacti are the best-known desert plants. But cacti don't live only in hot, dry places. While they are most likely to be found in the desert areas of Mexico and southwestern United States, they can be seen as far north as Nova Scotia. There are certain types of cactus that can live even in the snow.

Desert cacti are particularly good at surviving very long dry spells. Most cacti have a very good root system so they can absorb as much water as possible. Every available drop of water is taken into the cactus and held in its fleshy stem. A cactus stem can hold enough water to last for two years or longer.

The cactus may be best know for its spines. Although a few kinds of cactus don't have spines, the stems of most types are covered with these sharp needles. The spines have many uses for the cactus. They keep animals from eating the cactus. They collect raindrops and dew. The spines also help keep the plant cool by forming shadows in the sun and by trapping a layer of air close to the plant. They break up the desert winds that dry out the cactus.

Cacti come in all sizes and shapes. The biggest cactus in North America is the saguaro (sa-GWAH-row). It can weigh 12,000 to 14,000 pounds and grow to be fifty feet tall. A saguaro can last several years without water, but it will grow only after summer rains. In May and June, white blossoms appear. Many kinds of birds nest in this enormous cactus: white-winged doves, woodpeckers, small owls, thrashers, and wrens all build nests in the saguaro.

Directions: Answer these questions about cacti.

1. Where are you most likely to find a cactus growing? _Mexico and_
southwestern United States

2. How long can most cacti survive without water? _two years or more_

3. What are some ways the cactus uses its spines? _to keep animals from eating_
the plant and to collect water and keep the plant cool

4. What is the biggest cactus in North America? _saguaro_

55

Lizards

Lizards are reptiles, so they are cousins to snakes, turtles, alligators and crocodiles. Like other reptiles, lizards are cold-blooded. This means that their body temperatures change with that of their surroundings. However, by changing their behavior throughout the day they can keep their temperature fairly constant.

Usually, the lizard comes out of its burrow early in the morning. Most lizards like to lie in the sun to warm up before starting their daily activities. In the mid-morning, they hunt for food. If it becomes too hot, lizards can raise their tails and bodies off of the ground to help cool off. At mid-day, they return to their burrows or crawl under rocks for several hours. Late in the day, they again lie in the sun to absorb heat before the chilly desert night.

Like all animals, lizards have ways to protect themselves. Some types of lizard have developed a most unusual defense. If a hawk or other animal grabs one of these lizards by its tail, the tail will break off. The tail will continue to wiggle around to distract the attacker while the lizard runs away. A month or two later, the lizard will grow a new tail.

There are about 3000 kinds of lizards, and all of them can bite. But only two types of lizard are poisonous: the Gila (HE-la) monster of the southwestern United States and the Mexican beaded lizard. Both are short-legged, thick-bodied reptiles with fat tails. These lizards do not attack human beings and will not bite them unless they are being attacked by the human.

Directions: Answer these questions about lizards.

1. What does "cold-blooded" mean? _it means their body temperature_
changes with that of their surroundings

2. What can a lizard do if it becomes too hot? _lift its tail and body off the ground_

3. What part of the lizard can break off if the animal is caught by an attacker?
its tail

4. What two kinds of lizards are poisonous?
1) _the Gila monster_   2) _the Mexican beaded lizard_

56

Man In The Desert

Long before the white man came to live in America, Native Americans had discovered ways for living in the desert. Some of these Indians were hunters or belonged to wandering tribes that stayed in the desert for only short periods of time. Others learned to farm and live in villages. They made their houses of trees, clay, and brush.

The desert met all of their needs for life: food, skins for clothing, and materials for tools, weapons, and shelter. For meat, the desert offered deer, birds, and rabbits for hunting. When these larger animals were hard to find, the Indians would eat mice and lizards. Many desert plants, such as the prickly pear and mesquite, provide fruit and seeds that can be eaten.

The first white men to come to the desert were searching for furs and metals, such as silver and gold. These pioneers were usually unsuccessful at living in the desert. They found the great heat and long dry periods too difficult to live with. When they left, they left behind empty mining camps, houses, and sheds that have slowly fallen apart in the sun and wind.

Directions: Answer these questions about deserts.

Check √

1. The main idea is:
- ☑ Before the white man came to live in America, Native Indians had discovered ways for living in the desert.
- ☐ Some Indians were hunters or belonged to wandering tribes who stayed in the desert for only short periods of time.

Write

2. Who were the first humans to live in the desert? _Indians_

3. What did the Indians use to make their houses in the desert?
trees, clay, brush

4. What kind of food did the Indians find in the desert?
deer, birds, rabbits, mice, lizards, fruit and seeds from
desert plants

5. Who were the white men who came to live in the desert?
hunters and miners

57

Review

Camels are well suited to desert life. They can cope with infrequent supplies of food and water, blazing heat during the day and low temperatures at night, and sand blown by high winds.

There are two kinds of camels: the two-humped Bactrian (BACK-tre-an) and the one-humped dromedary (DROM-a-dare-ee). The dromedary is the larger of the two. It has coarse fur on its back that helps protect it from the sun's rays. The hair on its stomach and legs is short to prevent overheating. When camels **molt** in the spring, their wool can be collected in tufts from the bushes and ground.

The legs of the dromedary are much longer than those of the Bactrian. Animals that live in very hot countries tend to have longer legs. This gives them a larger area of body surface for heat to escape from. Bactrian camels live in the deserts of central Asia where winters are bitterly cold, so they are not as tall as the dromedary.

Both kinds of camel have pads on their feet that keep them from sinking into the sand as they walk across it. The camel's long neck allows it to reach the ground to drink water and eat grass without having to bend its legs. It also can reach up to eat leaves from the trees.

The camel does not store water in its hump, as many people believe. The hump is a fat storage. When there is plenty of food, the camel's hump swells and feels firm. During the dry season when there is little food, the fat is used up and the hump shrinks and becomes soft.

Directions: Answer these questions about camels.

Check √

1. The main idea is:
- ☑ Camels are well suited to desert life.
- ☐ There are two kinds of camels.

2. Based on the other words in the sentence, what is the correct definition for "molt"?
- ☐ gets sick
- ☑ sheds its hair
- ☐ becomes overheated

Write

3. List the two kinds of camels.
1) _Bactrian_   2) _dromedary_

4. Which kind of camel has one hump? _dromedary_

5. Why doesn't a camel sink into the sand when it walks?
because of special pads on its feet

58

82

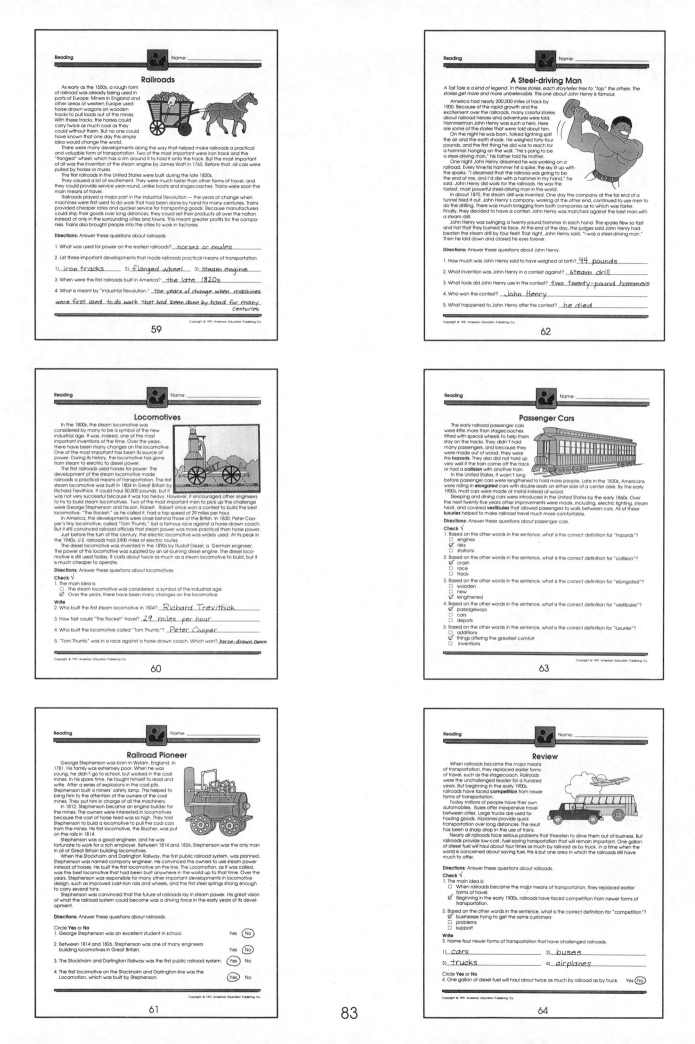

Reading Name: ______

Railroads

As early as the 1550s, a rough form of railroad was already being used in parts of Europe. Miners in England and other areas of western Europe used horse-drawn wagons on wooden tracks to pull loads out of the mines. With these tracks, the horses could carry twice as much coal as they could without them. But no one could have known that one day this simple idea would change the world.

There were many developments along the way that helped make railroads a practical and valuable form of transportation. Two of the most important were iron track and the "flanged" wheel, which has a rim around it to hold it onto the track. But the most important of all was the invention of the steam engine by James Watt in 1765. Before that, all cars were pulled by horses or mules.

The first railroads in the United States were built during the late 1820s.

They caused a lot of excitement. They were much faster than other forms of travel, and they could provide service year-round, unlike boats and stagecoaches. Trains were soon the main means of travel.

Railroads played a major part in the Industrial Revolution — the years of change when machines were first used to do work that had been done by hand for many centuries. Trains provided cheaper rates and quicker service for transporting goods. Because manufacturers could ship their goods over long distances, they could sell their products all over the nation instead of only in the surrounding cities and towns. This meant greater profits for the companies. Trains also brought people into the cities to work in factories.

Directions: Answer these questions about railroads.

1. What was used for power on the earliest railroads? horses or mules
2. List three important developments that made railroads practical means of transportation.

   1) iron tracks 2) flanged wheel 3) steam engine
3. When were the first railroads built in America? the late 1820s
4. What is meant by "Industrial Revolution." the years of change when machines were first used to do work that had been done by hand for many centuries

Reading Name: ______

Locomotives

In the 1800s, the steam locomotive was considered by many to be a symbol of the new industrial age. It was, indeed, one of the most important inventions of the time. Over the years, there have been many changes on the locomotive. One of the most important has been its source of power. During its history, the locomotive has gone from steam to electric to diesel power.

The first railroads used horses for power. The development of the steam locomotive made railroads a practical means of transportation. The first steam locomotive was built in 1804 in Great Britain by Richard Trevithick. It could haul 50,000 pounds, but it was not very successful because it was too heavy. However, it encouraged other engineers to try to build steam locomotives. Two of the most important men to pick up the challenge were George Stephenson and his son, Robert. Robert once won a contest to build the best locomotive. "The Rocket," as he called it, had a top speed of 29 miles per hour.

In America, the developments were close behind those of the British. In 1830, Peter Cooper's tiny locomotive, called "Tom Thumb," lost a famous race against a horse-drawn coach. But it still convinced railroad officials that steam power was more practical than horse power.

Just before the turn of the century, the electric locomotive was widely used. At its peak in the 1940s, U.S. railroads had 2400 miles of electric routes.

The diesel locomotive was invented in the 1890s by Rudolf Diesel, a German engineer. The power of this locomotive was supplied by an oil-burning diesel engine. The diesel locomotive is still used today. It costs about twice as much as a steam locomotive to build, but it is much cheaper to operate.

Directions: Answer these questions about locomotives.

Check √

1. The main idea is:
   - ☐ The steam locomotive was considered a symbol of the industrial age.
   - ☑ Over the years, there have been many changes on the locomotive.

Write

2. Who built the first steam locomotive in 1804? Richard Trevithick
3. How fast could "The Rocket" travel? 29 miles per hour
4. Who built the locomotive called "Tom Thumb"? Peter Cooper
5. "Tom Thumb" was in a race against a horse-drawn coach. Which won? horse-drawn coach

Reading Name: ______

Railroad Pioneer

George Stephenson was born in Wylam, England, in 1781. His family was extremely poor. When he was young, he didn't go to school, but worked in the coal mines. In his spare time, he taught himself to read and write. After a series of explosions in the coal pits, Stephenson built a miners' safety lamp. This helped to bring him to the attention of the owners of the coal mines. They put him in charge of all the machinery.

In 1812, Stephenson became an engine builder for the mines. The owners were interested in locomotives because the cost of horse feed was so high. They told Stephenson to build a locomotive to pull the coal cars from the mines. His first locomotive, the Blucher, was put on the rails in 1814.

Stephenson was a good engineer, and he was fortunate to work for a rich employer. Between 1814 and 1826, Stephenson was the only man in all of Great Britain building locomotives.

When the Stockholm and Darlington Railway, the first public railroad system, was planned, Stephenson was named company engineer. He convinced the owners to use steam power instead of horses. He built the first locomotive on the line. The Locomotion, as it was called, was the best locomotive that had been built anywhere in the world up to that time. Over the years, Stephenson was responsible for many other important developments in locomotive design, such as improved cast-iron rails and wheels, and the first steel springs strong enough to carry several tons.

Stephenson was convinced that the future of railroads lay in steam power. His great vision of what the railroad system could become was a driving force in the early years of its development.

Directions: Answer these questions about railroads.

Circle **Yes** or **No**

1. George Stephenson was an excellent student in school. Yes (No)
2. Between 1814 and 1826, Stephenson was one of many engineers building locomotives in Great Britain. Yes (No)
3. The Stockholm and Darlington Railway was the first public railroad system. (Yes) No
4. The first locomotive on the Stockholm and Darlington line was the Locomotion, which was built by Stephenson. (Yes) No

Reading Name: ______

A Steel-driving Man

A Tall Tale is a kind of legend. In these stories, each storyteller tries to "top" the others. The stories get more and more unbelievable. This one about John Henry is famous.

America had nearly 200,000 miles of track by 1900. Because of the rapid growth and the excitement over the railroads, many colorful stories about railroad heroes and adventures were told. Hammerman John Henry was such a hero. Here are some of the stories that were told about him.

On the night he was born, forked lightning split the air and the earth shook. He weighed forty-four pounds, and the first thing he did was to reach for a hammer hanging on the wall. "He's going to be a steel-driving man," his father told his mother.

One night John Henry dreamed he was working on a railroad. Every time his hammer hit a spike, the sky lit up with the sparks. "I dreamed that the railroaa was going to be the end of me, and I'd die with a hammer in my hand," he said. John Henry did work for the railroads. He was the fastest, most powerful steel-driving man in the world.

In about 1870, the steam drill was invented. One day the company at the far end of a tunnel tried it out. John Henry's company, working at the other end, continued to use men to do the drilling. There was much bragging from both companies as to which was faster. Finally, they decided to have a contest. John Henry was matched against the best man with a steam drill.

John Henry was swinging a twenty-pound hammer in each hand. The sparks flew so fast and hot that they burned his face. At the end of the day, the judges said John Henry had beaten the steam drill by four feet! That night, John Henry said, "I was a steel-driving man." Then he laid down and closed his eyes forever.

Directions: Answer these questions about John Henry.

1. How much was John Henry said to have weighed at birth? 44 pounds
2. What invention was John Henry in a contest against? steam drill
3. What tools did John Henry use in the contest? two twenty-pound hammers
4. Who won the contest? John Henry
5. What happened to John Henry after the contest? he died

Reading Name: ______

Passenger Cars

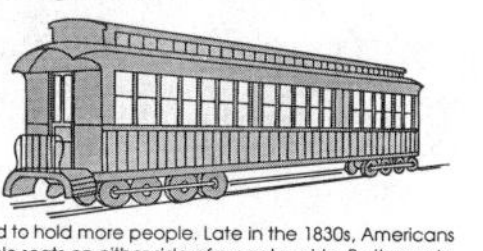

The early railroad passenger cars were little more than stagecoaches fitted with special wheels to help them stay on the tracks. They didn't hold many passengers, and because they were made out of wood, they were fire **hazards**. They also did not hold up very well if the train came off the track or had a **collision** with another train.

In the United States, it wasn't long before passenger cars were lengthened to hold more people. Late in the 1830s, Americans were riding in **elongated** cars with double seats on either side of a center aisle. By the early 1900s, most cars were made of metal instead of wood.

Sleeping and dining cars were introduced in the United States by the early 1860s. Over the next twenty-five years other improvements were made, including, electric lighting, steam heat, and covered **vestibules** that allowed passengers to walk between cars. All of these **luxuries** helped to make railroad travel much more comfortable.

Directions: Answer these questions about passenger cars.

Check √

1. Based on the other words in the sentence, what is the correct definition for "hazards"?
   - ☐ engines
   - ☑ risks
   - ☐ stations
2. Based on the other words in the sentence, what is the correct definition for "collision"?
   - ☑ crash
   - ☐ race
   - ☐ track
3. Based on the other words in the sentence, what is the correct definition for "elongated"?
   - ☐ wooden
   - ☐ new
   - ☑ lengthened
4. Based on the other words in the sentence, what is the correct definition for "vestibules"?
   - ☑ passageways
   - ☐ cars
   - ☐ depots
5. Based on the other words in the sentence, what is the correct definition for "luxuries"?
   - ☐ additions
   - ☑ things offering the greatest comfort
   - ☐ inventions

Reading Name: ______

Review

When railroads became the major means of transportation, they replaced earlier forms of travel, such as the stagecoach. Railroads were the unchallenged leader for a hundred years. But beginning in the early 1900s, railroads have faced **competition** from newer forms of transportation.

Today millions of people have their own automobiles. Buses offer inexpensive travel between cities. Large trucks are used for hauling goods. Airplanes provide quick transportation over long distances. The result has been a sharp drop in the use of trains.

Nearly all railroads face serious problems that threaten to drive them out of business. But railroads provide low-cost, fuel-saving transportation that will remain important. One gallon of diesel fuel will haul about four times as much by railroad as by truck. In a time when the world is concerned about saving fuel, this is but one area in which the railroads still have much to offer.

Directions: Answer these questions about railroads.

Check √

1. The main idea is:
   - ☐ When railroads became the major means of transportation, they replaced earlier forms of travel.
   - ☑ Beginning in the early 1900s, railroads have faced competition from newer forms of transportation.
2. Based on the other words in the sentence, what is the correct definition for "competition"?
   - ☑ businesses trying to get the same customers
   - ☐ problems
   - ☐ support

Write

3. Name four newer forms of transportation that have challenged railroads.

   1) cars 2) buses

   3) trucks 4) airplanes

Circle **Yes** or **No**

4. One gallon of diesel fuel will haul about twice as much by railroad as by truck. Yes (No)

OVERVIEW

ENRICHMENT READING is designed to provide children with practice in reading and to increase students' reading abilities. The program consists of six editions, one each for grades 1 through 6. The major areas of reading instruction--word skills, vocabulary, study skills, comprehension, and literary forms--are covered as appropriate at each level.

ENRICHMENT READING provides a wide range of activities that target a variety of skills in each instructional area. The program is unique because it helps children expand their skills in playful ways with games, puzzles, riddles, contests, and stories. The high-interest activities are informative and fun to do.

Home involvement is important to any child's success in school. *ENRICHMENT READING* is the ideal vehicle for fostering home involvement. Every lesson provides specific opportunities for children to work with a parent, a family member, an adult, or a friend.

AUTHORS

Peggy Kaye, the author of *ENRICHMENT READING*, is also an author of *ENRICHMENT MATH* and the author of two parent/teacher resource books, *Games for Reading* and *Games for Math*. Currently, Ms. Kaye divides her time between writing books and tutoring students in reading and math. She has also taught for ten years in New York City public and private schools.

WRITERS

Timothy J. Baehr is a writer and editor of instructional materials on the elementary, secondary, and college levels. Mr. Baehr has also authored an award-winning column on bicycling and a resource book for writers of educational materials.

Cynthia Benjamin is a writer of reading instructional materials, television scripts, and original stories. Ms. Benjamin has also tutored students in reading at the New York University Reading Institute.

Russell Ginns is a writer and editor of materials for a children's science and nature magazine. Mr. Ginn's speciality is interactive materials, including games, puzzles, and quizzes.

WHY ENRICHMENT READING?

Enrichment and parental involvement are both crucial to children's success in school, and educators recognize the important role work done at home plays in the educational process. Enrichment activities give children opportunities to practice, apply, and expand their reading skills, while encouraging them to think while they read. *ENRICHMENT READING* offers exactly this kind of opportunity. Each lesson focuses on an important reading skill and involves children in active learning. Each lesson will entertain and delight children.

When children enjoy their lessons and are involved in the activities, they are naturally alert and receptive to learning. They understand more. They remember more. All children enjoy playing games, having contests, and solving puzzles. They like reading interesting stories, amusing stories, jokes, and riddles. Activities such as these get children involved in reading. This is why these kinds of activities form the core of *ENRICHMENT READING*.

Each lesson consists of two parts. Children complete the first part by themselves. The second part is completed together with a family member, an adult, or a friend. *ENRICHMENT READING* activities do not require people at home to teach reading. Instead, the activities involve everyone in enjoyable reading games and interesting language experiences.

ENRICHMENT ANSWER KEY
Reading Grade 5

Page 65   1. portable 2. scribble 3. telephone 4. phonograph 5. microscope 6. automatic 7. prescription 8. photograph 9. biology; biography

Page 66   *Top row:* This room is very cold. I'm shivering from the cold. *Middle row:* The furnace is worthless. I have a very small memory. *Bottom row:* I always liked the way you look. Don't try to be funny.

Page 67   *Underline:* raining cats and dogs, getting on my nerves; scaredy cat; shoot off your mouth; got my goat, face the music; on a wild goose chase; Hold your horses; call it a day; chicken out; wire-haired, darts in his eyes, rip me off, up to; knees knocking together; suddenly became sunny, a hard time, horsing around, Scared the pants off, in two winks; results and pictures will vary

Page 68

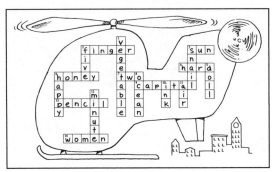

ENRICHMENT ANSWER KEY
Reading Grade 5

Page 69 1. c 2. b 3. c 4. a 5. b

Page 70 1. E, C 2. E, C 3. C, E 4. C, E 5. C, E
6. E, C

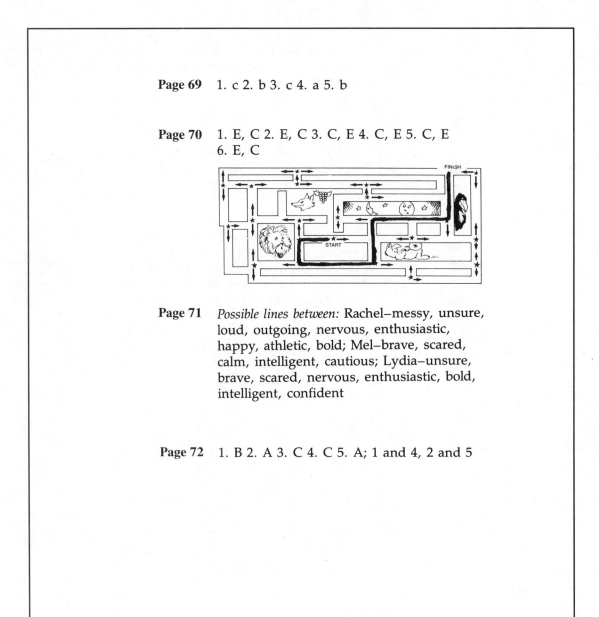

Page 71 *Possible lines between:* Rachel–messy, unsure,
loud, outgoing, nervous, enthusiastic,
happy, athletic, bold; Mel–brave, scared,
calm, intelligent, cautious; Lydia–unsure,
brave, scared, nervous, enthusiastic, bold,
intelligent, confident

Page 72 1. B 2. A 3. C 4. C 5. A; 1 and 4, 2 and 5